Joseph Judson Taylor
THE GOD OF WAR

Joseph Judson Taylor

THE GOD OF WAR

SPINEBILL PRESS

To the memory of
A Brother Beloved
Minister of the Gospel
RYLAND READ TAYLOR
1858-1887

Spinebill Press
Katoomba NSW, Australia
spinebillpress.com

A catalogue record for this
book is available from the
National Library of Australia
NATIONAL LIBRARY OF AUSTRALIA

ISBN 978-0-6455948-4-3

Design and typography by Michel Streich
Typeset in Caslon and Korolev

Contents

Foreword

The general theme which I have undertaken to present in the following pages is not new. For centuries it has engaged the minds of earnest men, and has deeply stirred their hearts. Naturally it has evoked divers and dissonant views, and not infrequently it has aroused deep feeling. The war god appeals to human passions.

The views herein set forth are the result of studies that have extended intermittently through thirty years, and of work similarly through four. They are deliberate, kindly, mature, and neither inflexible nor final. As the tide of recent passion recedes, and men come to realize the mischief that has been done, they may be willing to consider any honest effort to find a better way.

I had it in mind to give a list of authors to whom I am indebted, and of their works on which I have drawn, but on looking over the list I find that it contains three hundred names and more, the number of books being larger; and so I shall save labour and space by leaving them out. Several have been quoted directly, both because it serves my purpose better to have them speak in their own way and because their honoured names give weight to the truths they have uttered. Others have been duly credited by name with sentiments which I have chosen to express in my own words, but always with strict loyalty to the import of what they said.

Such as it is, this little volume is sent forth with the devout desire that it may confirm in the faith of the gospel the hearts of all who name the name of Christ, and that through their renewed fidelity to the truth it may hasten the day when the demon of hatred and deadly strife shall be driven from the whole world and men of all nations and tongues shall be brought into brotherhood and into peaceful and happy harmony with the will of God, as it is set forth in Jesus Christ.

J. J. T.

I

Among the Gods

The existence of the divine and eternal in contrast with the human and temporal is not a matter for argument. Conviction does not lie at the end of a course of investigation instigated by a desire to search out the causes of things. It comes by intuition. It arises spontaneously. It grips the emotions and sentiments of the race with unfailing power.

Research has discovered tribes without architecture or art, without coins or codes of law, without recognition of natural relations, without any of the institutions and inventions that mark social progress, but never a tribe without the idea of the divine, out of which somehow comes a demand for the worship and service of rational creatures. In Africa, it is said, there was found a group so low in the scale of intelligence as to acknowledge no god, but in the same breath they confessed that they prayed to the skies. Among all primitive peoples prayer is before investigation. Ethnology knows no race devoid of religious emotions and religious exercises.

This universal experience is an invincible proof of godhood. With authority that cannot be ignored the instincts of the race assert the existence of the divine, and declare there is a god or gods. The sacred books of the nations never enter into any formal discussion on this point. They simply assume the divine existence, and proceed to state and enforce the duties which it implies.

The records of all primitive peoples, whether ancient or modern, indicate a belief in gods more than one. The first divine name mentioned in the Bible is plural. If literally rendered the opening sentence of the Old Testament would run: "In the beginning gods created the heavens and the earth." By the same rule: "Gods said, Let there be light, and there was light; gods saw the light that it was good, and gods separated the light from the darkness." Throughout the entire creation story gods are doing the work. In the end gods said: "Let us make man in our image, after our likeness," as if there were more than one engaged in the making. Some scholars call it the plural of majesty or fullness; others find in it the idea of the trinity, but in any case the word is plural, and this is the point under consideration.

The oneness of the true God was made known to man by revelation. Moses said: "Hear, O Israel , the Lord thy God is one Lord; and thou shalt love the Lord thy God with all thy heart and all thy soul and all thy might." It was a matter of divine disclosure rather than of human discovery. Amid scenes of deep solemnity God, who assumed the existence of other beings called by the divine name, forbade the recognition of any god other than himself. He gave further command that there should never be made any graven image or likeness of anything in heaven above or in earth beneath as an object of worship and service.

With such commandments clearly before them the chosen people found difficulty in visualizing God and holding communion with him. He seemed like an evanescent glory without form or local habitation. He was to them a vast shadowy something shrouded in clouds and darkness, uttering no voice and showing no outline of his person, and from such a presence timid souls shrank away abashed. They yearned for a god who approached their own sphere of existence and passed within the range of their comprehension, and the yearning became a temptation to disobey the law which they had received. Under stress of desire for an easy worship they said unto Aaron: "Up, make us gods to go before us."

Called of the Lord, they yet made a calf in those days, and danced with delight before the work of their own hands. Rebuke and entreaty, threatening and punishment were not sufficient to deter them from their evil ways, and they forsook the Lord and served the gods of the heathen among whom they dwelt. They took up the tabernacle of Moloch, and the star of the god Remphan; they made groves in high places, and rendered their devotions to strange gods. More than a hundred times do the Scriptures record their iniquity in scorning the commandment and offering their devotions to other gods.

The New Testament declares that there is one God and Father of all, who is above all and through all and in all; but it gives recognition to other beings called by the divine name. Paul the apostle says there are gods many, as there are also lords many; and he applies the term to Satan, as the god of this world.

Summing up the Scripture teaching on the subject early Christian students, the eminent Augustine among them, held that heathen divinities were real, but were evil in nature. As late as the seventeenth century there were devout and scholarly men who contended that the sacred books of the heathen were corrupted forms of divine revelation, the Bible only being the true word of God.

To this day there are some who regard all the great religions of the race as having a divine origin and divine elements, Christianity surpassing them only in the degree of its excellence. To this day also men of backward races hold to the doctrine of many gods. In a public address in Asheville, North Carolina, in 1916, the Rev. S. G. Pinnock, a missionary to Africa, said he found difficulty in impressing the natives with the idea that there is but one true God; they said one might be enough for white folks, but negroes had to have more.

In his natural and unaided weakness man has never been able to reach the conception of a god large enough to establish his throne in the heavens and thence to rule over the entire realm of created things. The ancient Phenicians were unable to rise to such an idea. The wisdom of Babylonia and Egypt fell short of it. The fervid faiths of Athens and Rome, taught by priests and augurs of high degree, knew nothing of such a being. The noblest efforts of unaided devotion rose only to a great Zeus or a mighty Pan, who heldthe supreme place and ruled in the highest, but had various minor divinities beneath him and under his control to aid in governing the universe and working out the administrations of time.

By such a scheme Pluvius was set over the clouds, Neptune over the seas, Ceres over the grain fields, Pluto over the lower regions, and so on to every realm of divine providence and human interest. There were also gods to regulate the variant appetites and passions of men. It was a convenient division of labour and responsibility. It afforded opportunity to distribute divine honours and at the same time to lighten divine burdens. It was not an exclusive arrangement, however. In any great enterprise the gods were at liberty to work together, and this they sometimes did.

The scheme necessarily provided a god of war. The history of mankind is a story of strife, man against man, family against family, nation against nation, race against race. In the matter of organized effort nothing has ever made so great demands upon the resources of the race as has the practice of war. Naturally the god who reigns over a realm so vast and important is a being of great power and influence. His reality is attested by every consideration that demonstrates the existence of the Creator himself. He is known by his works done in all ages and nations, and by his sway over the lives of men in every land.

Like the God of Peace, the god of war has different

names according to the advancement of his devotees or the languages which they speak. Some writers state that before the time of the Trojan war Belus had conquered the island of Cyprus and other adjacent territory; and they identified the conquering Belus with the Phoenician Baal, whose power had overthrown the Hittite kingdom at an earlier date.

Egyptian legends tell of the exploits of Sesostris, who led armies of archers and charioteers; and the first of her written laws recognize the war god, and make provision for his service in the support of warriors and in the honour accorded them. Professor Morris Jastrow, of Pennsylvania University, says ancient Egypt recognized some thirty gods of war, or in the stress of conflict called upon all the gods of the pantheon for assistance. The chief of her war gods, however, was Sutek, surnamed the Golden, and counted on to give victory over all enemies. Relying on Sutek's power, Pharaoh issued the haughty challenge: "Who is Yahweh (translated Jehovah), that I should obey his voice to let Israel go? I know not Yahweh, neither will I let Israel go."

Before the days of Moses Hammurabi gave distinct recognition to Marduk or Merodach, the war god of Babylonia, whom he proudly called his father. He made the name of the great god the centre of his legislation, and trusted him for power to overcome his enemies. In a famous inscription discovered in modern times he says: "I am Hammurabi, the mighty king, king of Kadingirra (Babylon), the king whom the regions obey, the winner of victory for his lord Merodach. Thenceforward I am Hammurabi, the mighty king, favoured of the great gods. With the might accorded me by Merodach I built a tower with great entrances, whose summits are high."

In the native mythology, Marduk or Merodach was represented as originally a sun god, who ruled over the forces of nature, breaking the rigours of winter and bringing in the beauties of spring, as in the beginning he had broken the powers of darkness and had brought order out of chaos. As Babylon became ambitious of power and began to extend her dominions into a vast empire, the god who had given prosperity in times of peace was invoked for the exigencies of war, and his guidance was sought in the direction of armies and the slaughter of foes.

With the acquisition of riches and power through conquest the desire for more burned in the hearts of the people, and the god who granted the fulfillment of the desire rose to a higher place in popular esteem. In the end other qualities fell into abeyance, and Marduk was honoured as the great god who had given them dominion over the nations round about. He had also Bel as an able and honoured ally in his bloody work.

After Babylon became subject to Assyria Marduk retained some measure of his former glory. For a long time Assyrian rulers were inducted into office with a ceremony called Taking the Hand of Marduk. An ancient inscription, quoted by Prof. L. von Ranke, recording the overthrow of Babylon's king and the conquest of the land, states that after the victory Cyrus did reverence to Bel-Merodach. It was an effort to appease the anger of the war gods of the conquered realm. Jeremiah the prophet, who honoured only one God, mentioned the overthrow of Belshazzar and his godless associates in these words: "Babylon is taken, Bel is confounded, Merodach is crushed."

The chief war god in Assyria was called Asshur, the name signifying strength and leadership. In the earlier records he was simply the patron divinity of the capital city, which bore his name. In the beginning of his career he disclosed no vicious and bloody traits; but as the people grew in wealth and influence they also grew in their greed and arrogance, and were filled with desire to possess the things of others. They wished a place in the sun, and they turned to the chief god of the realm for aid in their unholy schemes.

They set Asshur over the national armies; and as victory followed their efforts, they gave him the supreme place in the pantheon. Lesser divinities gradually dropped into obscurity, or else they were endued in fancy with warlike qualities, and made mere satellites of the great war god. It was Asshur that "thrust the king of Babylon into a consuming fire and ended his days." All victories were ascribed to his will. He was represented by the figure of a strong man armed and bearing a winged disk, the disk suggesting the glint of sunlight on burnished armour and the wings indicating rapidity of movement.

Hosea the prophet recognized his existence, but scorned his power. Noting the ills that afflicted Israel and foreseeing greater ills to come he warned the people against trusting the native god of war: "Asshur shall not save us, neither shall we ride (to victory) on horses."

Among the gods of India Seeb or Siva, the god of destruction, red with the blood of unnumbered dead, held a high place. At different times he took different forms, but his favourite guise was that of the demon Bhairava, whose ornaments were garlands of serpents and a necklace of skulls. He had power to loose the forces of desolation and to breathe pestilence into the air. He was grim of visage and frightful of form, and he moved among the children of men, causing them to blanch with apprehension and tremble with fear.

The old Norse mythology named the war god Odin or Woden, and assigned him the fourth day of the week. In the opening of his career he was merely a man of immense strength, a sort of brute man, mighty in body, dauntless in spirit, terrible in battle, a genuine hero of the primal sort. About him the admiration of the old Norse heart gathered, rising higher and higher until it broke forth in adoration and made him divine.

Under the sway of Odin Teutonic peoples began to count brute force and physical courage the supreme virtues. Through the centuries they cherished that base conception, and gloried in the gory deeds of Attila and Charles Martel and Charlemagne and Peter the Hermit and their successors in brutality down to the present time. They esteemed the service of the barbaric war god the noblest form of human activity, and felt that they had been robbed of their heritage if they were not allowed to die in battle.

Sometimes, as the natural signs of decay appeared, they inflicted wounds upon their own bodies with the idea of disclosing the warrior spirit and winning a more abundant entrance into the presence of Odin, who made it a virtue to subdue all forms of fear and march forward without a tremor into the jaws of violent death. In the great Valhalla, which lay just beyond the field of blood, the war god awaited his faithful servants, and welcomed them to the victory feast according to the heroism of their deeds, while those who died a natural death were debarred from the joys of the festal board.

The dead heroes were feasted on the flesh of the wild boar in the presence of Odin; the supply was inexhaustible, for the boar which was cooked every morning was made whole every night. The drink for the banquet of the mighty was mead made from the milk of the sacred goat, and they drank it from the skulls of their slaughtered foes. The banquet of he hog and strong drink was entirely suited to the appetites of the red-blooded men who gathered there.

When not feasting the gallant warriors were graciously allowed to continue their favourite earthly pursuit, being better fitted for that than for anything else. Every day they rode forth in glittering array to butcher one another; but at meal-time they were duly healed of their wounds, and were called back to their favourite feast. It was a brutal conception, but it had the virtue of consistency at least. Certainly it did not present the absurdity which some preachers have lately proclaimed, that men who hate and kill one another in battle are welcomed to the Better Land, where they forget the animosities which they have cherished and the wounds and deaths which they have inflicted, and together praising the Prince of Peace

"Bring forth the royal diadem,
And crown him Lord of all."

In Greek the supreme war god was called Ares. He was accounted the son of the great Zeus and the spiteful Hera, the two corresponding respectively to Jupiter and Juno of the Latin mythology. In the earlier times Ares was not esteemed the source of war, or the manager of camps and campaigns; rather he represented the wild rage and destructive violence displayed on the field of battle. Homer represented him as the model warrior of the heroic age, fully armed with gleaming helmet and bronzed cuirass, embossed shield and glittering spear, going forth with the familiar strut to be the scourge of mortal men. He inherited a vicious and turbulent spirit, and delighted in confused noise and garments rolled in blood. Unlike many who send others to battle, he did not spare himself.

According to the Greek myths he twice engaged in personal encounter with Hercules. In the first instance the combat was ended by a bolt of lightning from the great Zeus, but in the second he received an ugly wound, his opponent being aided by Athena, who bore him a ceaseless grudge. Later he sought to punish the goddess for her opposition, but the effort was not to his honour. Homer said of the incident: "Giving back somewhat she seized with strong hand a stone that lay upon the plain, black, rugged, huge, which men of old had set to be a landmark; this she hurled, and struck the impetuous Ares on the neck, and unstrung his limbs. Seven rods he covered in his fall, and soiled his hair with dust, and made his armour ring."

"It was evidently a surprise to his gay lordship. Then did brazen Ares bellow loud as nine thousand warriors, or ten thousand, cry in battle, as they join in strife and fray." The bruised god took the case up to Olympus; but the supreme Zeus said: "Nay, thou renegade, sit not by me and whine. Most hateful art thou of all the gods that dwell on high Olympus. Thou ever lovest strife and war and battle. Truly in thee thy mother's spirit is intolerable. " His mother also rebuked him as lacking in moderation and judgment, and he was dreaded even among the gods.

Once he fought with Halirrhotus, who had invaded his home and seized his daughter Alcippe. He vanquished the invader, and was tried and acquitted by a court of the gods sitting on the Areopagus. It was an early case of the application of the unwritten law, gods and men alike being accorded the right to defend their homes.

In the earlier representations Ares was burly and bearded, stern of feature and fully armed, ready at all times for grim and savage work. Later he was set forth in more attractive form, having a smooth face and curly hair, a figure more pleasing to Aphrodite and others of the softer sex, whom he tempted from the paths of virtue.

Usually he travelled in a chariot made by his sons Panic and Fear, who also attended him as he rode forth to incite the passions of war and direct the movements of cruel men. His train was completed by the presence of Eris the goddess of strife, Enyo the goddess of fury, Keres the goddess of death, and a contingent of bloodthirsty demons prepared to roam over the battle-fields and bear the dead away. His symbols were a spear and a torch, suggesting the general character of his work. The creatures sacred to him were the vulture and the dog, that feed on filth. Especially at Thebes and also at Athens he with his paramour was worshipped in bloody and elaborate rites.

The Romans called him Mars. They accounted him the father of the warlike founder of their city, Rhea Silvia being his consort. They accorded him high honour, rendered him deep devotion and trusted him for ceaseless care. They conceived him to be stately in form, majestic in mien, stern in character, pitiless in spirit, but not essentially vindictive or needlessly cruel. His dress, adorned with belts and buckles, straps and tinsel, became the model for the soldier of all time. He rode in a stately chariot drawn by Terror and Fear and driven by a distracted woman holding a torch in her hand. He bore a shield on his arm and a spear in his hand, and they were said to have fallen down from heaven.

In the Roman calendar Mars was honoured in the name of the first month of Spring. At that time his dancing priests marched through the city bearing the sacred shield and sounding the war trumpets which bade the armies abandon their winter quarters and take up their work of carnage and destruction. Under his grim guidance the conquering eagles were carried over all Gaul and across the seas to the Ultima Thule. In Roman thinking Mars ranked second only to the great Jupiter himself, and became the patron deity of the city and the empire. As Rome ruled the world the war god assumed the supreme place in the pantheon, and in some important respects he has kept it to this day.

Through centuries of carnage all the base passions of the human soul have risen up and raged in power, but they have not for an instant dimmed the glory of the war god. Men who have retired to their quiet laboratories away from the sickening scenes of war and have devised the deadly explosives and the fearful fixtures that grind together in one bleeding and repulsive mass the flesh of men and mules call upon the god of war for aid in their wicked work. History records no case in which warring peoples have failed to call upon the god of battles for his blessing on their bloody deeds.

Recent German writers deeply stirred the wrath of their enemies by confident appeals to a god capable of approving such crimes as German soldiers committed. In German writing, however, all nouns begin with a capital letter, and it seems that those devout Germans did not make their supplications to the God of the whole earth, who loves all his children alike; rather they made their appeal to their "old Ally," the German god of war. In a published article Burris A. Jenkins, formerly president of Transylvania University, made reference to certain aspects of German teaching in these words: "The only god possible under it is the god of the Hun, the god of battles, the god of a Teuton, a tribal and heathen god, a sort of Woden or Thor." President Faunce also suggested that the god of militarism is necessarily provincial.

With such a god in mind Professor Kaeler represented the German armies as having four fronts, three toward the enemy and one toward heaven. Another German author spoke of a divine form standing before the German people, as Jesus stood before the grave of Lazarus, and calling them to renewed energy in fighting for the fatherland. Throughout the empire loyal ministers of religion devoutly offered their daily prayers to the German Gott, almost frantically imploring his aid in their efforts to butcher the people of other lands.

Failing to note the difference between the German Gott and the God of the whole earth, destined shortly to bruise Satan under the feet of the saints, one of our own religious teachers said: "It shocks and disgusts all reverent souls to read the German Emperor's blatant claim to partnership with God, God being the junior member of the firm. It is blasphemous to think of the God of grace and mercy as being in sympathy with the mad lust of power and the murderous disregard of human life which has marked the German conduct of the war."

Strangely enough the same eminent teacher proceeded to urge that in the critical times in which he wrote "every house of worship ought to be open continually," and that "our good people ought to repair to the sanctuary to lift up their hearts and their voices in earnest and importunate prayer for the blessings of the Most High on our cause." Earnest and importunate prayer for a mightier might to smash the German might! It was our cause against the German cause, and our God against the German Gott.

In the same spirit a circular letter was sent out from a group of persons calling themselves a committee on national preparedness appealing to ministers of religion throughout the country. It said in part: "This insolent god-claiming attitude of the German Emperor our people treat with silent contempt or utter indifference, but it is just here that a serious mistake is being made by us. We are permitting this blasphemous propaganda to fall upon the minds of our whole population without offering any active opposition to its acceptance." With a suggestion that scruples might arise "even among many religious men in the army," the authors of the circular proceeded to urge ministers "as an act of religious patriotism and justice" to use their pulpits "to counteract this evil" and "to destroy this sacrilegious propaganda."

In harmony with the request some ministers proceeded to preach and to pray in terms quite as provincial and profane as anything heard in England or Germany. Before a great assembly a preacher of prominence addressed a god whom he considered capable of sinking into hell entire nations, not even sparing godly women and innocent children. In his rage and vituperation he prayed: "O god, help the man on the ship, who aims the cannon, to send to hell a submarine every time one sticks its dirty stinking nose above the water. O god, damn Germany and Turkey and all the rest of that gang of thugs and cutthroats. O lord, I don't want to bless them, and you can go ahead and damn them just as soon as you get ready, so far as I am concerned. But, god, don't wait too long. Hurry up, and help us."

Such a prayer was rightly addressed to a provincial god who had no interest in the people the preacher wanted to kill and send to hell. It was never a prayer we have known and loved.

Another offered the following bitter petition, which was widely circulated through the religious press: "God in heaven, forbid that any man or woman in this land should be so steeped in sin, so morally leprous with the taint of Germanism, so rotten-souled from vile contamination with these vile criminals as ever by a single thought to favour, peace until down in the dust of unconditional surrender the forces of hell acknowledge the power of heaven, and until the criminal German leaders swing high from the gallows, which though doing their appointed work would still be contaminated by the dead bodies of those lying, looting, outraging beasts, whose crimes would sicken a tiger!"

With more dignity and reverence another distinguished man addressed a god who was supposed to regard the interests of a particular nation, and he prayed in part in these words: "That thou wilt come to the men who are already on the front, to General Pershing and the men who are under him, and to the men in training in France and on the high seas, our men in camps in training here and those subject to call, those on the way to camp and those who may be called for land service or sea service. God, grant them thine own strength and thine own direction.

"For the navy we pray that thou wilt give wisdom and guidance to Admiral Sims and to all those under him. God, grant unto our soldiers and our sailors the abiding conviction that they are fighting in the name of liberty, of righteousness, of brotherhood and of humanity. Give to them, we pray thee, that vision which shall sustain them throughout the long weary hours of fighting or waiting, of enduring or suffering. God, give to them the spirit that cannot be broken. God, give to them the perseverance and the resolution which never dreams of defeat and ever claims the victory in advance."

In all these utterances whether of emperor or editor, evangelist or teacher, preacher or publicist, the same spirit is shown. Whether by instinct or purpose none of them mention the name of Jesus, who forbids violence and commands non-resistance and love. All alike appeal to a provincial god, who in each case is supposed to favour one class of his creatures in their fell desire to hurt and to kill and to destroy others of the same blood and so to fill the world with additional bereavement and woe. Each assumes that such a god will side with him and against those whom he wishes to destroy, or even to send to hell. Nowhere is there any touch of the humility that admits the possibility of error in the petitions that are made. Nowhere a "nevertheless, not as I will." It is a distinct recognition of the god of war, and it may be traced through the ages from the myths of ancient Babylonia and Egypt to the theology of modern Europe and America.

Current thinking makes no mistake in the matter. The men who have reported from foreign battlefields need no interpreter when they speak of trailing the war god. A popular poet touches a responsive chord in the following lines:

"The war god has gone through the wheatfields,
    And eaten the children's bread;
He has gone through the beautiful orchards,
    And all the trees are dead;
He has gone through the whole wide world,
    Like a dragon that must be fed.

How shall we speak to the war god,
    And what shall the message be?
For never a prayer we have known and loved
    Will be heard by such as he.
For him there is no word of praise,
    Nor any psalmody."

In glowing periods orators have declaimed on the passing of the war god. They have pointed to the advance civilization the progress of learning, to the instincts of humanity, the demands of economy, to the sentiments of brotherhood, to the dictates of reason, to the entire range of rational considerations, and they have demonstrated that all these forbid the foul art of war. Peace societies have been formed, well officered and highly financed. Peace agents have traversed land and sea, dispensing fine phrases and gathering millions of money. Poets have rhymed about the silencing of the war drum, the gathering of nations fraternal parliament and all kindreds and tongues federated for the enforcement of perpetual peace. Prophets have foretold the time when the soldier and the husband-man shall come together, and shall beat their swords into plowshares and their spears into pruning hooks, nation no longer desiring to lift sword against nation, neither to learn war any more. Angels have stooped over simple shepherds pasturing their quiet flocks, and have filled the vibrant air with songs peace on earth and good will to men.

These all have caught the popular ear and have moved the popular heart. But the god of war has looked on derision and his followers have heard with scorn which they have felt no care conceal. They have seen the orators who grew rich by preaching peace suddenly adding to their wealth by preaching war. They have seen peace societies struck dumb in the presence of mobilizing armies. They have seen peace agents who quietly smoked in the shadows of the Hague blaze into fire at the call to war. They have heard peace poets adding a new fervour to their song as they told of the glories of war. They have seen the prophets of peace cower before the haughty stride of the defiant militarist and reserve their Christmas sermons till after the war. They have calmly allowed the orators to declaim, and the peace agents to smoke their pipes, and the poets to indulge their pleasing rhymes, and the prophets to tell of the dawning day, and the angels to sing their melodious songs. Confident in the war god's power they know full well that in due time the basilar passions of men will assert themselves, the voice of reason will be drowned, the holy sentiments of the human heart will be trodden under foot, the covenants of righteousness will become paper scraps, the gates of Janus will be thrown open, the dogs of war will be let loose and the minions of hell will go forth in renewed strength to work desolation and death among the children of men.

II

The War God Honoured

The god of war is honoured in the honours accorded his servants. "Inasmuch as ye have done it unto the least of these, ye have done it unto me." By this unfailing rule he is the most popular divinity known to the race. All classes and kindreds have rendered him their tribute of praise.

In times so remote that their history lives only in myth and legend the men who successfully served the war god were given uncommon honour. Ancient Persia and Egypt fostered the spirit of adoration for conquerors, while yet they lived. The Ptolemys succeeded to the Egyptian throne, and claimed at once the double allegiance due to such as combine in one the character of both god and king.

In Homer's day men distinguished in battle became the people's idols. Alexander of Macedon went out from the temple of Ammon a veritable son of god, and was adored by the Persians as a being divine. The legendary founders of Rome were sons of Mars and Rhea Silvia, and their infancy was guarded by divine providence guiding the shepherd and the she wolf. Julius Cæsar coveted a place among the celestials; after the battle of Pharsalia he was ranked as divine, and his statue in the temple on the Quirinal was inscribed to the invincible god. Later he was called Jupiter Julius, and in due time the senate gave permission for his name to be set among the nation's divinities. Sextus Pompey claimed to be a son of Jupiter, and the claim was conceded by many of his admirers. Octavius assumed a divine parentage; after the battle of Actium godlike qualities were accorded him, and he was called a son of Jove.

Through all the far-off times the glory of the war god rested upon his servants. It included the right and the might to rule, and it justified the cruelties which rulers so often inflicted on their helpless subjects. The historic barbarities of military discipline rest at last on the authority of the war god. The divine right of kings lies in the assumption that the king as a son of god can do no wrong.

Men distinguished with the title Great have invariably been men of blood, who ruthlessly crushed out the lives of their fellow-men. In the pitilessness of ravening beasts they went forth butchering hapless peoples without mercy and without remorse, and they impressed the ages with their name and fame. Such were Ptolemy, Cyrus, Darius, Alexander, Pompey, Herod, Constantine, Charles, Otho, Peter, Frederick. These and such as these, high priests in the service of the god of carnage and destruction, won the homage of their own times and also of succeeding centuries.

Only less honoured were others less conspicuous in the same service: Cambyses, Nebuchadnezzar, Sennacherib, Xerxes, Epaminondas, Lysander, Cyrus the younger, Scipio, Antony, Titus, Attila, William the Bastard, Richard 1, Wallace, Robert the Bruce, Wallenstein, Cromwell, Napoleon, Wellington, Nelson, von Moltke, Garibaldi, and others a mighty host.

Some of these men were crafty, cruel, drunken, envious, lustful, unjust, utterly lacking in the cardinal virtues that mark true manhood in the walks of peace; only in the foul art of war were they distinguished above others, but that distinction overshadowed and obscured their abominable iniquities in private life and marked them as objects of popular praise. Others of them were men of blameless reputation in morals, but they wrote no book , contrived no invention, established no public policy, founded no institution, headed no reform, advanced no ruling idea, made no great speech, and yet by their zeal and success in serving the war god and accomplishing the butchery of their fellow-men they rose above the masses of mankind and found place in the halls of fame.

Whatever their prospects for the world to come the minions of the war god easily win the honours of the present time. Among presidents of the United States Washington, Jackson, Taylor, William Henry Harrison, Grant, Hayes, Garfield, Arthur, Benjamin Harrison, McKinley and Roosevelt held military titles, while Monroe, Tyler, Pierce and Buchanan knew something of military service. Other men known as fighters have been put forward by minority parties seeking to gain the great office by making the blood appeal to the popular franchise.

English law excuses a butcher of animals from jury

service in capital cases, lest the man of blood fail to enter into the finer sentiments of the human heart; but the human butcher is lauded and praised, and is set apart for the special prizes of citizenship. Even the illiterate man, too stupid and indolent to read the simplest primer, is accorded the high privilege of the franchise, if only his grandfather fought in some war! In popular esteem the disciple of the war god outranks the disciple of Christ, other virtues being just the same.

Touching this matter J. L. M. Curry forcefully says: "Public sentiment is so perverted that military service is regarded as the all-sufficient qualification for any office or position; and no rewards, pecuniary, professional, civil, are adequate compensation for having been connected directly or remotely, usefully or as a drone, with an army. Marlboro had special Parliamentary grants, gifts from the queen, marriage portions for his daughters, presents of costly plate, two and a half per cent. on the pay of foreign troops supported by England, fifty thousand pounds per annum, and various court sinecures and pensions for his wife. Wellington, whose blindest admirers would not ascribe him qualifications for such a part, was called to form a cabinet, and gave his great influence to monopoly and intolerance. 'A little more grape, Captain Bragg' and 'General Taylor never surrenders' became shibboleths to fire the popular heart and set a successful soldier above the tried political experience and tested statesmanship of Daniel Webster and Henry Clay.

"Far above any possible or conceivable attainment

in any other walk of life does the furor over military service put soldiers and sailors. Commissions, peerages, pensions, grants, decorations, lucrative posts for heroes and their wives and families! The inventor of the Congreve war rocket received a pension of $6,000, while Humphrey Davy, the inventor of the miners' safety lamp and the author of priceless discoveries in anesthetics and electricity, received no state reward whatever."

All the forms of literature glorify the war god in glorifying his servants. The earliest ballads sang of mighty heroes, who were fearless in battle. Vergil's immortal epic opens its stately measures with the words: "*Arma virumque cano*," and it is a characteristic case. Apart from arms and the slaughter which they inflict not many men are able to attract the masters of majestic hexameters, but in that service common clay is easily cast into heroic mould. In the smoke of battle foul iniquities are hidden from the sight of human eyes. In the noise of the strife memory is dulled, and soldiers' sins sink into oblivion.

The public press is true to form, when it announces the names of those killed in the effort to kill others as Our Heroes. The cold form of a dead disciple of the war god awakes the muse and incites the poet to sing:

"No useless coffin confined his breast,
Nor in sheet nor in shroud we wound him;
But he lay like a warrior taking his rest,
With his martial cloak around him.

We buried him darkly at dead of night,
The sod with our bayonets turning,
By the flickering moonbeams' misty light,
And the lantern dimly burning.

Slowly and sadly we laid him down,
From the field of his fame fresh and gory;
We carved not a line, we raised not a stone,
But left him alone with his glory."

The obscure victim expelled from home and forced to die on a foreign field of blood evokes a song:

"Duty's demand in full he paid;
Our own his dauntless life did yield;
Our own he fell on Flanders field;
His life on homeland's altar laid.

O'er him the winds unheeded sweep;
And green the kindly grasses grow;
And often gentle breezes blow,
And loving friends at home do weep."

The lyrics of all lands find place to honour the servants and victims of the war god, whether six hundred or six thousand who ride a bloody sacrifice into the jaws of death. Music set to the measured tread of marching thousands awakens swelling emotions in the hearts of men in every clime.

History is largely a story of the wars which states

and nations have waged. In the brief annals of our own land, which loudly proclaims its love of peace and its aversion to war, the pages devoted to each respectively offer a striking comparison. The number recording the struggles of war far exceeds that portraying the triumphs of peace.

In the broader annals of older nations thousands of pages, hundreds of thousands , tell the story of ambition and folly, of tragic error and seething passion, displayed by men who have bowed at the shrine of the war god, and have arisen to go forth in blind rage destroying art and industry, happiness and progress, accumulated treasure and priceless life; but through the entire record there glows the splendour of a heroism which thrills the heart centuries after the suffering actors have passed from the sanguinary scenes and dropped into the silence.

No story of farmers toiling to feed the hungry world, of merchants struggling to distribute their needed goods, of philosophers grappling their profound problems, of physicians risking their lives to relieve suffering, of ministers of religion striving against the enemy of souls, stirs the emotions of men as do the stories of Leonidas holding the pass against the invading hosts of Persia and of Horatius keeping the bridge against the hordes of Lars Porsena. Such exploits quicken the pulses of the dullest men.

Biography also bears ample witness to the glory of the war god. Alexander closed his brief career in debauchery and shame more than two thousand years ago; but after the lapse of the tardy centuries he holds the public eye, and men are studying his life anew, and some are trying to set him among the benefactors of the race.

Julius Cæsar was a base and vicious man. He was feared and hated by those who knew him best. In open day he was set upon and killed by men who had been accounted his friends. But his exploits in the service of Mars made him a place among the notables of all time. To this day youths can hardly be inducted into the treasures of classic lore without entering by way of Cæsar's Commentaries on the Gallic Wars.

William of Normandy, history avers, was cruel, harsh, insolent, lustful, vindictive, unjust. He also permitted his soldiers to indulge the most violent excesses, sparing neither age nor sex, beauty nor virtue in their mad career of license and lust. In his own family his cruelties did not abate, and it is said that he beat his wife to death with a piece of harness. But he was an ardent devotee of Odin, a robber of princes and kings; and to this day there are some who think it a thing of honour to trace their history back to so base an origin.

Against his own father Richard I entered into a conspiracy with Philip of France. Paternal love forgave the crime. The base ingrate renewed the treachery, and drove the devoted father from his possession into a distant land, where he died in humiliation and shame. But Richard valiantly served the god of war, and ignoring the fact that the lion is a pitiless beast of prey men endeavoured to honour him and his god by calling him Richard of the Lion Heart.

Robert the Bruce betrayed his compatriot Wallace to his English enemies. He saw him brought before a hostile court and duly convicted of treason, homicide, sacrilege, robbery and arson. On the day Wallace was convicted of robbery and homicide he was hanged. For burning churches his body was dismembered, and his entrails burned. For being a traitor, as adjudged by the honourable court, his head was displayed on London Bridge, and parts of his mangled body were suspended from gibbets in different parts of the country. Robert, it is said, witnessed and approved it all; but he was a mighty man in the bloody work of war, and his other crimes went into eclipse. Now the story of Robert the Bruce properly touched up is considered suitable literature to shape the character of the youth of the land.

Eulogists declare that Napoleon was a bundle of contradictions, ready to profess any creed or to promulgate any opinion, a gloomy and peculiar prodigy, a sceptred hermit wrapped in the solitude of his own originality. He trampled Europe under his feet as ruthlessly as behemoth tramples the reeds by the river's brink, but he was a mighty warrior. Taking up Voltaire's sneer about the god who is on the side of the heaviest battalions, he valiantly served the same; and to this day his name is esteemed in Paris and throughout France as that of no other man. Where sin abounded the glory of the war god abounded more.

In recent months books about war have been the chief commodities of the trade. Stories of battles have filled columns of newspapers and magazines. None of them have told the unbiased truth in its fullness and power. They have held the gruesome aspects of the theme in abeyance or have ignored them entirely, and have rather exploited the heroism and glory of war. The public censor saw to it that the soldiers suffering in the filth of the camp or the squalor of the battlefield did not speak out of their own hearts.

The din of battle stirs the souls of men, even when they share the peril. In early life Washington expressed an inclination to arms. After a skirmish in which he had taken part he said: "I heard the bullets whistle, and, believe me, there was something charming in the sound." He esteemed it an honour that four balls had passed through his coat and two horses had been killed under him while he was serving with Braddock.

Others have found similar charm in the detonation of military ordnance and in the shriek of deadly missiles. Regardless of the havoc and death, the subsequent judgment and fixed destiny of immortal souls in whose interest Jesus suffered on the cross, ministers of religion have sometimes urged men into war, where prepared or unprepared they are swept into vast eternity by thousands and tens of thousands. In some instances they seem willing to butcher the enemy simply as a pastime.

Lately Mr. W. T. Ellis, who has given some evidence of being a Christian, made it a business to trail the war god abroad and to make report to papers with which he was connected. In the prosecution of his work he recited this incident: "All to the music of the big guns and for my edification the artillery fired, after it had been explained in its concealed dugout, the General himself attending. We sent out three shells into the German reserves four miles away, also six shrapnels, in the space of forty-five seconds. It was an ear-splitting, but highly interesting, private rehearsal I hope it messed up the enemy some."

Honoured by the General's personal attention and the gracious enlightenment accorded him concerning the mysteries of the deadly war device the Christian man lately from his Sunday-school lessons felt himself edified by the private rehearsal. He enjoyed the attention, and his joy was heightened by the hope that his entertainment resulted in the death of some stranger four miles away.

Another cheerful correspondent gave this account: "I sat listening to the rumble of the guns. Not for three consecutive seconds was there a cessation in the firing, and the great variety of angry tones told that the chorus came from artillery of almost every kind known to modern warfare. Between the rattle of the small stuff and the roar of the heavies a vast range of man's most destructive genius was represented. One with a musical ear and a thorough knowledge of scales might have been able to set those tones into an inspiring score, though for its execution the world would have to fashion instruments unknown to any existing orchestra."

The next description is worthy of the Teutonic war god himself: "The symphony of the artillery began to sound, beating up and up in terrible roarings. The sky precipitated steel, and shivered the fragments into line. The air above became palled with the fleecy smoke of exploding shrapnel, and the earth was threshed with iron hail. The infantry lay on its face and laughed. They made bets on the accuracy of the firing and the explosive quality of the shells. Meanwhile the artillery was doing its job, and doing it mighty well. It had a reputation to sustain, and in that case it lived up to its past. The guns smashed at the foe with devastating effect, examining the line with cool care of accuracy; and when they found things to hit, they hit with the might of Thor's hammer. Every machine gun was turned on at full tap. It was like cutting down hay. Before that furious fire rank after rank of the opposing host went sinking down to the earth to rise no more. It was glorious slaughter. Over the field, under clouds of shrapnel, out from the deep drifting smoke battalions of men were running forward, falling down, firing, rising and running forward again, worming their way through woods and bushes to get on the firing line. And hidden by the hills the brisk cannon were pumping off shells as fast as the eager gunners could work the pieces."

Amid such scenes the devotees of the war god broke forth into singing: "They drove irresistibly forward through fields and coppices, drove singing and clattering through nodding villages, sweeping up the enemy outposts with the unhesitant and decisive onslaught of men who delighted in their work. When they were not firing, they were making jokes about the enemy; when they were neither firing nor joking, they sang. Sometimes they sang as they fired. They sang lustily, and sang a song that the enemy heard. It was a great day." And it reflected great honour on the god of war, who directed it all. Either side may equally honour the war god. "The enemy stormed with all the power of their artillery, all the might of their rushing hosts. Under the shelling our trenches were battered to mud, were blown into big explosions, so that many soldiers were entombed. The trenches were searched by shrapnel from end to end. Death ran riot in the pits. The first regiment lost seven hundred. The second was shredded to tatters. Neither gave way. The men fought like demons, and fought to the last gasp; but they did their noble work." It was the work of killing and being killed. Their rage and bitterness held them to the last gasp, and they died fighting.

"The strength of the wolf is the pack;
The strength of the pack is the wolf."

The battle continued: "The dense mass of the enemy attack was coming on with a rush, when the little Maxim ceased firing, the whole crew lying dead about the gun. At once a big private jumped from the firing line. In a flash his strong arm had lifted the piece, tripod and all, and he was running to the bridge head, where he planted the gun in the face of the foe. Absolutely alone he sat down, and his nimble fingers raced the fully charged belt through the fatal machine. Under that jet of death the advancing column wavered, and then broke for cover in the fields, leaving scores of dead that the stammering gun had laid low. As the last man vanished, the big soldier fell forward on the gun dead, pierced by many a ball."

The performance showed equal valour on either side, and was a high tribute to the war god. The poet heard a song in every missile of death:

"I come from the ether, cleft hotly aside,
Through the air of the soft summer morning;
I come with a song, as I dash in my pride;
It's a dirge, and a message of warning.

No sweet idle dreams, no romance of love,
No poet's soft balm-breathing story
Of armour-clad knights at tournament gay,
But a flag, and a field that is gory.

Swift hurled from the gun 'mid volumes of smoke,
I crash, a grim messenger flying;
Before me the living; behind me, alas,
leave but the dead and the dying."

Writers who ardently oppose the war god and all his works bear him reluctant tribute. Mr. H. G. Wells, the English pacifist, says: "There is no denying that war brings out almost incredible qualities of courage,

44

devotion and individual romance, which do not appear in the suffocating times of peace."

One of the interesting books born of the big war was the letters of Christine Cholmondeley, who was a music student in Germany when the war began. She pays this tribute to the warrior: "The emperor stood by himself in front of the others. He was very grave with a look of solemn exaltation. He was royalty in all its most impressive trappings, a prince of the fairy tales, splendidly dressed, dilated of nostril, flashing of eye, the defender of homes, the leader of glory, the object of the nation's worship and belief and prayers become visible and audible to thousands who had never seen him before, and had worshipped him only by faith. It was as though the people were suddenly allowed to look upon God. There was a profound hush. Even I, rebellious and hostile to the whole attitude, sure that the real motives beneath it all were base, and constitutionally unable to care about Kaisers, was thrilled. His speech was wonderfully suited to the occasion. All the great reverberating words were in it, the big words ambitious rulers have conjured with since time began: God, Country, Duty, Hearth, Home, Wives, Little Ones, God again, lots of God. See in fancy the great crowd quiet, struck into religious awe, crying quietly, men and women like little children gathered at the feet of a heavenly Father. 'Go to your homes,' said he, dismissing them with uplifted hand; 'go to your homes, and pray.' They went in dead silence. Quietly, like people going from church; moved, like people going from communion." It was a marvellous tribute to the war god.

The war god is glorified also in the great monuments of the world, chief of which are erected to his votaries. The only statue of Julius Cæsar that has been preserved stands in the vestibule of the Pantheon in Rome. Probably the most elaborate and costly monument ever raised to man is that of Victor Immanuel II, which stands near the ruins of the Coliseum looking down the street through which he rode at the head of his victorious armies in 1871, when he came in to rule over a united Italy. Other great monuments to warriors may be seen in every great city of Europe. Without their monuments to soldiers London and Paris would be stripped of their chief ornaments. Boston and New York, Philadelphia and Baltimore, Washington and Richmond glorify war in their monuments to men who were leaders of armies.

Further honour is awarded the war god in elaborate festivities. In Babylon there were feasts to Marduk, as there were to other divinities. Similar honour was accorded Asshur in Assyria and Ares in Greece. While the recent orgy of blood was desolating the nations, and hapless women and children were dying of hunger, the god of war provided elaborate feasts for his devotees in camp.

A gifted correspondent described one of those typical festivities in these words: "The dinner, by a nameless regiment at a nameless point, was altogether the jolliest stag party in which I ever shared. It was held in a mess hall, which was a dugout with a roof of logs and stones and earth several feet thick, and seating fifteen persons, but with no space for waiters to pass behind chairs.

"It was a good dinner, with both turkey and roast pig for meats, and there was great chaffing directed at the chaplain of the mess. Of course, ran the jibes, the priests know about the good things of life and can get food when soldiers starve.

"Though he was unmercifully tormented upon all the weaknesses of the cloth and his own failings, from his anxiety over his young beard his ambition for captain's stripes, the radiant priest was prouder of that dinner than of any sermon he had ever delivered; and he was happy be man and an equal among men instead of cossacked 'papa' among peasant women and children."

All jolly tribute the grim god of war, as priests of Baal feasted at Jezebel's table while Israel perished with hunger.

The War God a Saviour

Great in name, celebrated in story and song, glorified in literature, immortalized in monuments and honoured in elaborate festivities the god of war is accorded yet a higher place as a saviour. According to his admirers his service enhances the value of the soil itself, builds the body, ennobles the character, exalts the ideals of life, vindicates humanity, atones for national sins, redeems civilization and finally saves the soul of the individual.

Speaking of those who died in battle an ardent admirer of the service said: "By watering it with their blood they have made the soil more precious to every human being that walks upon it." Quite a reassuring statement, since all blood is just alike. It is said that God has used but one kind of blood for men everywhere. The blood shed on either side of the recent conflict was equally precious and equally sanctifying to the ground; so if the idea set forth is correct, the soil is a good deal dearer than it was before the recent sacrifice of ten millions or more of the world's best citizens.

Advancing a step Secretary Baker, whose utterances have something like official authority, speaks of the influence of the war on character in these impressive terms: "When the war is over and men and women of America have had opportunity to obtain a true perspective on its conduct and results, there will be an adequate appreciation of Dr. Odell's statement about Camp Hancock: 'I would rather intrust the moral character of my boy to that camp than to any college or university I know.'"

The statement was not intended to reflect on the colleges and universities of the land, but to glorify, the value of camp life. Other camps were also under the Secretary's control, and there is no reason to believe that they were less effective than Camp Hancock in conserving and developing the moral character of the young men who were forced into training.

Likewise one of the army officials gave this assurance to parents whose sons had been drafted into the service: "Whether your boy is a private or an officer, you can rest assured that he will come out a manlier man. He will have more self-reliance, be more courageous, and will display a greater quality of fair play and justice." This on the assumption that he comes out, otherwise the helpless parent can think about how much more precious the soil is made by the dead boy's blood.

Similarly one of the great dailies that regularly echoed war sentiments from a safe distance said: "The over-indulged boy at first feels distressed over the absence of home comforts, but in the open-air life, in the substantial food, in the morning and afternoon exercises, he builds up his system. The flaccid muscles become taut, sunken chests expand, troubled lungs assume a healthful state, and under the observant eye of the government man-maker the boy soon emerges from the shadows into the sunlight of perfect manhood." Exactly. How fine!

Results so excellent are not confined to this country, but other lands have enjoyed the blessing. Sir Robert Armstrong Jones, an English knight, saw resulting from the war increased sobriety, better care of babies, and a healthier public sentiment generally.

Across the Rhine a Teuton writer stated the case in these impressive terms: "War is the noblest and holiest expression of human activity. For us too the great glad hour of battle will strike. Still and deep in the German heart must live the joy of battle and the longing for it. Let us ridicule to the utmost the old women in breeches who fear war, and deplore it as cruel and revolting. No; war is beautiful. Its august sublimity elevates the human heart above the earthy and the common."

Probably the Teutons express the idea with more vigour than some others, but they are by no means alone in the notion that war is beneficial to nations. Europeans generally seem to feel that it is a sort of national purgative, which gives a stronger tone to national life and character. Long eras of peace, they think, tend to soften the tissue of the people and render them effeminate, while war hardens and glorifies. The plain people who are the chief victims of war usually feel that life is hard enough, but they are not generally consulted on the subject of war; the ruling classes hold the reins, and bring on the catastrophe.

Men who sometimes profess hatred of war are constrained to admit its beneficial results. A minister of the Gospel lauds the service in these impressive terms:

51

"War has kindled the spirit of patriotism among the peoples engaged has spread spirit of sacrifice throughout all the world which must be a benediction for ages to come." Especially does feel that for their loss life and treasures accumulated through years of toil England and France and America will come into richer experiences and more abundant life.

Under the power such teaching a poet inspired to sing the praises of war to the disparagement of peace in these fervid lines:

"Oh, we were pleasure blinded then,
And we were trivial thinkers, too;
We were but children dressed as men,
With only childish things to do.

We had no high resolves to keep;
The splendours of our past had paled;
Our souls were dull with drowsy sleep,
And as a race we'd failed.

The Prussian hordes assailed the truth,
And tyranny with all its might
Challenged the temper of our youth,
And manhood blossomed in a night.

Then on a crimsoned foreign land
Our race won back its pristine pride;
For liberty it took its stand,
As long ago the fathers died."

Further, Mr. Roosevelt, whose name suggests Teutonic blood, touches the theme with characteristic scorn: "There is a Dr. Jekyl and Mr. Hyde in nations as well as individuals, and sheer terrorism is often found working hand in hand with flabby and timid pacifism for the undoing of righteousness and for the deification of the most brutal forms of militarism. The blood and iron statesman of one nation finds in the milk and water statesman of another the man predestined through the ages to be his ally and tool. The universal and all-inclusive arbitration people, and most of the men and women who have taken the lead in the pacifist movement in this country during the last five or ten years, are preaching international cowardice. The college boys who adopt professional pacifist views, who make peace leagues and preach the doctrine of international cowardice, are unfitting themselves for any career more manly than that of nursery maid."

The same forceful writer credits war with establishing religion in Asia and Africa and Europe: "Christianity is not the creed of Asia and Africa solely because in the seventh century Christians in Asia and Africa, in addition to being rent asunder by bitter sectarian animosities, had trained themselves not to fight, whereas the Moslems were trained to fight."

Further he proceeds to say: "If the peoples of Europe in the seventh and eighth centuries and on to the seventeenth had not possessed a military equal to and gradually growing superior over the Mohammedans who invaded Europe, at this moment Europe would be Mohammedan, and Christianity would be extinct."

According to this distinguished writer the god of war is also a god of religion, who has used the same method to establish Mohammedanism in Asia and Africa and Christianity in Europe; and judged by their fruits both are violent and bloody, and every man is at liberty to take his choice.

The Rev. J. M. Moore, of Brooklyn, advances a step farther, and speaks of war god service as making atonement for national sins and in some way saving what he calls the nation's soul. It seems that at one time Germany offered Belgium national integrity and also indemnity for damage done in passing through her territory, but had the offer met with rejection and a determination to fight. Referring to Belgium's part in the incident Preacher Moore says: "By her decision she wiped out the blot of Leopold's hateful reign and memory, and took her place with old Greece and Palestine."

Dr. Moore makes his statement quite on his own responsibility. In Belgian annals there is no hint of repentance for Leopold's atrocities in Africa, nor any indication of a desire to repudiate either him or his deeds. It seems that she did take her place with old Greece and Palestine, both rankly heathen.

In the same strain Dr. Moore proceeds: "She had to submit to vandalism that humanity elsewhere might be vindicated. Belgium will have lost everything. The material damage, the destruction of cities and villages, the total collapse of industry and trade are incalculable. The damage done to the monuments, sacred to art and religion, is not only incalculable, but irreparable. The suffering inflicted on millions of people baffles imagination, but the moral and spiritual gain is equally, inestimable. Belgium will have proven to the world her determination and her right to exist as a free nation. She will have won the sympathy and the admiration of the whole world. She will have left an inspiring example to posterity. She has lost everything, but she has saved her soul."

Rising to still nobler heights the war god is said to have his Calvaries. Referring to the Verdun battle-field, where so much blood sanctified the soil, an ardent Christian said: "Sad it was to see the surrounding hills blasted and covered with 300,000 graves. Verdun is indeed the Calvary of France, for there France was crucified for all civilization."

In the same strain one of the officers said: "Then came the great hour when Christs, however humble and wherever found, heard the call to man the barricades of freedom." He explained that previously: "We could not understand it, the broken Christs who climbed Calvary for the sake of others." Under the spell of it all a minister of the Gospel said: "Not the Son of God alone, but millions of his children were being crucified, that the sins of the world might be washed away."

Men of ability and standing freely expressed the opinion that those who died on the battle-field as truly died for mankind as did Jesus himself . One of the great dailies reported a Professor in a Christian school as saying: "Christ was the Saviour of the world, but the world is not yet saved. Our boys in the war are making up for what is lacking in the Saviour's work."

In view of all these great things accomplished through war it is not strange that a poet breaks forth in this fervid song:

"Oh, I'm surely glad I'm living,
And sharing in the fight!
And the blood o' me is tingling
With rapture and delight.

For the little tasks of peace times
Didn't wake me open-eyed;
And the safe and easy pathways
Left my soul unsatisfied.

Here's the biggest job that's happened,
Since the human race began:
We are making this world over,
As a decent place for man.

And I'm mighty glad I'm in it;
'Tis the thing that I should ask:
To be one of those partaking
In the world's supremest task."

In all this there is no sort of denial that God furnished the raw material, so to speak. He created the heavens and the earth, but it was without form and void; and he left it to the war god and his servants to finish the task, and make the world just right.

The war god's supreme glory, however, is found in being a saviour of souls. Mohammedanism distinctly teaches that every man killed in battle thereby secures the favour of Allah and an abundant entrance into his presence. The great Arabian said: "Whosoever falls in battle, his sins are forgiven; at the day of judgment his wounds shall be resplendent as vermilion and odorous as musk, and the loss of limbs shall be supplied by the wings of angels and seraphim." It was a pleasing prospect to set before the soldier at his bloody task.

In the recent strife the Germans made much of the Mohammedan idea. Their junkers and preachers solemnly assured the men at the front that in dying for their country they inevitably won a glorious reward on high. The German Gott, their old ally, could not deny eternal happiness to such as made the supreme sacrifice for the Fatherland. Holding the popular view that all soldiers killed in battle are heroes they said: "In the cloud palace sit the heroes."

The same doctrine was widely proclaimed in England. Both in print and in public address it was taught that men killed in the effort to kill their country's enemies went straight to heaven. Donald Hankey, the popular student in arms, said to his men: "If you are wounded, it is blighty; but if you are killed, it is resurrection." He made special mention of incorrigibles in the ranks: "One by one death challenged them. One by one they looked into his grim visage, and refused to be dismayed. They had been lost, but they had found the path home;

and when at last they laid their lives at the feet of the Good Shepherd, what could they do but smile?"

Captain Hankey was widely quoted, greatly admired and earnestly endorsed.

The same doctrine was taught in France. Harry Lauder, who lost a son in the strife, said: "I talked with men for hours at a time about their experiences in battle; but the one thing that I came away with above all other impressions was the conviction that every single one of those men, no matter what manner of life they had lived before, now possessed a calm and clear conviction that if he fell in battle he would pass into the life beyond."

In Belgium Cardinal Mercier stated the case in these impressive words: "If I am asked what I think of the eternal salvation of a brave man who has conscientiously given his life in defense of his country's honour and in vindication of violated justice, I shall not hesitate to reply that without any doubt whatever Christ crowns his military valour, and that death accepted in this spirit assures the safety of the man's soul. 'Greater love hath no man than this, that a man lay down his life for his friends.' And the soldier who dies to defend his brothers and to defend the hearts and altars of his country reaches the highest degree of charity."

Being a distinguished functionary of his church, the Cardinal spoke officially for Catholicism not only in Belgium, but also in Germany and other lands. His utterance was widely approved, and when he visited this country Brown University showed him distinguished honour.

The same doctrine was accepted in Canada. In the midst of the turmoil a reliable reporter gave this account: "Many churches turned their services into regular recruiting meetings for the army. They became merely one of the many agencies for prosecuting the war, and many a recruit was assured in so many words that should he be killed that very experience would gain for him an abundant entrance. Worked to the limit were the words of the Lord, 'Greater love hath no man than this, that a man lay down his life for his friends.'"

Among us the doctrine was earnestly preached. Leading religious bodies, knowing full well that the war would cost the lives of thousands who made no sort of profession of Christian faith, warmly endorsed it, and committed their people to the work of destruction. In different denominations men of prominence publicly taught that death in battle entitled the victim to eternal salvation.

Speaking to a body of soldiers, Dr. N. D. Hillis, of Brooklyn, said: "In a moral universe a just and loving Father will make up to a boy who sacrificed his all here, and will cause the supreme sacrifice to be worth while." Also Dr. Lyman Abbott, at one time minister in the same pulpit, said: "We may be sure that whatever their faults or their transgressions here the righteous Father will not refuse those heroic cross-bearers the crown of righteousness."

Another minister said: "Any young man who from a sense of duty gives his service to the war, and loses his life, will go to heaven. There is no other place for him to go." Another not quite so sure sets the thought in a question: "Can we believe that the soldier killed in the hell of battle is hurled into an endless hell?"

The questioner evidently expects a negative answer. In Turkey, Austria, Germany, France, Belgium, England, Canada and the United States it is practically the same. The idea widely prevails that the service of the war god saves. A Baptist minister puts the case in these words: "If any of our boys die in the war, they die a Calvary death, and on the third day they will be raised again; and if they have been faithful, they will be crowned with immortality."

A mission leader also spoke of the "self-denying love of the soldier boys in giving their lives for the redemption of the world"; and a mother whose son was among the conscripts complacently compared herself to "God who gave his only begotten Son," as recorded in John iii. 16.

Ten millions or more of mature men were destroyed in the war. Uncounted thousands of them went without repentance, without faith, without goodness, without preparation of any kind. Rather with cursing and bitterness they died in the effort to hurt and destroy their fellow-men. At most the stake in the issue was merely a form of human government. If such service was sufficient to save them and take them home to glory, there no place for the doctrine of atonement through the blood of Christ. If it did not save them, and many believe that did, they have been misled by ministers of religion, and are lost forever.

It is an appalling thing to contemplate. If the blind lead the blind, shall not both fall into the ditch?

The War God's Pleas

Honoured as the war god is, his service is so wasteful of property and life, so destructive of art and commerce and all the things that indicate the progress of the race, that he usually inspires his servants with some sort of excuse for any particular war which he leads them to undertake. When in the course of human events it is judged necessary for a people to enter into war with all the base passions which it engenders, as thousands go forth to kill and to be killed, "a decent respect for the opinions of mankind requires that they declare the causes which impel them" to such a course, though the course has been taken many a time without regard to popular opinion. In many instances the reasons are not formally stated, but are made to appear in the course of events.

1. In times very remote conquest constituted a mighty plea for war. It appealed to personal ambition for glory acquired through extended territory, increased resources, and added luxury and power. The strong coveted the possessions of the weak, and they proceeded to steal openly and by violence.

Nebuchadnezzar sent forth his armies and brought weaker peoples into subjection, until his dominion extended from the Euphrates to the Nile, and constituted one of the greatest empires known to the ancient world. His capital lying four-square, surrounded by a wall great and high, entered only through massive gates, watered by a river flowing through the midst, and adorned with all the beauty which wealth and power could contrive, became a symbol of the New Jerusalem coming down from God out of heaven. Within the walls the temple of the war god was roofed with cedar and overlaid with gold, while other divinities had their appropriate temples and shrines. Walking in his palace in the pomp of his pride the king disclosed the motive that had impelled him in all his work of spoliation and accumulation: "Is not this great Babylon which I have built for the house of my kingdom by the might of my power and for the glory of my majesty?"

He wanted a place in the sun. He wanted to make his name famous. He had the power to subjugate his weaker neighbours, and he used it with unflagging energy and remorseless cruelty. Marduk filled him with the spirit of conquest, and he went forth plundering and to plunder.

The wars of Cyrus the Elamite were born of the same rapacity. That ruler was called and chosen of God only as an instrument for restoring the Israelites to their native land, and re-establishing them in the heritage of their fathers; apart from that he was a true servant of the war god, under whose sway he spent his days. His rape of Persia and Media, Babylonia and Lydia, the last comprising the greater part of Asia Minor, was but the expression for his lust for conquest.

Favoured of his favourite divinity he found his chief joy in fighting and preparing to fight. In his later years he selected for himself the title King of the World, and in pitiless violence he tried to justify the name. Having a large part of Asia under his feet he planned to invade Africa, but grim death cut him down in the midst of his crimes.

The Persian invasions of Egypt under Cambyses and of Greece under Darius and his son Xerxes were not justified by existing conditions. Those rulers were merely filled with the robber spirit; and finding themselves in a condition to seize the property and power of adjacent states they marched forth to do their bloody work. Vain and unscrupulous they became pliant slaves of the war god, who sent them forth to drench the earth in blood.

The book of Esther throws an interesting side light on the character of Xerxes, called Ahasuerus. If there were no other record, his despotic and lustful temper would be fully established. His reckless and licentious deeds marked the decline of the Persian empire, and in the end brought down ruin upon his own head. He was murdered by two of his attendants, Aspamitres his chamberlain and Artabanus the captain of his guard. His violent death furnished a fit sacrifice to the war god whom he ardently served.

In moving Philip of Macedon against the cities of Greece, and later against Persia, the war god offered different pretexts; but back of the whole piratical course of that famous marauder was the robber spirit, which aroused him to covet and seize the wealth and power which belonged to others. He desired, and he purposed and planned to take by force. He also was struck down by the hand of an assassin, but his unholy schemes were passed over to his son and successor, who if possible was more unscrupulous and greedy than the father.

With Greece in subjection Alexander soon entered upon a campaign of spoliation and plunder, which extended far into Africa and on into Asia. It was a mad career of domination and desolation, which ended in a drunken debauch in distant Babylon. The idea that he was preparing the way for the coming of Christ by the spread of Greek culture or by anything else that he did is a curious and baseless fancy. It was preparation only in the sense that all previous events led up to that culmination in the world's history. The god of war was never interested in the coming of the Prince of Peace.

Through successive centuries the war god appealed to the spirit of conquest, arousing the avarice of rulers and kindling the cupidity of subjects, that armed forces might crush opposition and possess the things of others. No doubt there was personal rivalry between Pompey and Cæsar, but deeper than any feeling of personal antipathy was the desire to become the chief citizen of Rome and of the world, and to possess the power and luxury which such a position would impart.

Cæsar was not alone in being ambitious. That spirit followed on and infected others who worshipped at the same shrine. Napoleon felt it. In France he brought order out of chaos; but when he aspired to order other countries, he was feared and hated. What seemed good for France did not seem so good for other lands, and by the same violence which he had employed Napoleon was defeated and overthrown only seven years before the predestined end. It was greed against greed.

Most of the wars which we as a people have waged have had a similar origin. Whatever their immediate occasion, our early wars with the Indians were essentially wars of aggression and conquest. In the exceptional cases in which the forms of exchange involving a proper compensation were observed the principles of justice were often forfeited, and might or shrewdness set the standard of right. We wanted their lands; we took them, and drove the possessors out.

Speaking of the second Seminole war, typical of many, Roosevelt says: "As was usually the case in Indian wars, there had been wrong done by each side; but in that case we were the more to blame, although the Indians themselves were far from being harmless innocents. The Seminoles were being deprived of their lands in pursuance of the general policy of removing all Indians west of the Mississippi." Touching the ending of the strife he further says: "The great Seminole leader, Osceola, was captured only by deliberate treachery and breach of faith on our part."

Our war with the adjacent republic of Mexico originated in the same spirit. Be it assumed that Texas had the right to follow the lead of a Tennessean in seceding from Mexico, under whose liberal policies she had so greatly prospered, and then later to become a member of the American Union, she did not have the right to alienate from the sister republic territory along the Rio Grande which was not hers.

On that point Silas Wright said Texas had ceded territory on which she had no just claim and over which she had no rightful jurisdiction. The Mexican minister in Washington protested against the aggression in the most solemn manner, but protested in vain. When Mexico resented the aggression, we declared war against her. While it raged, we seized other Mexican territory in New Mexico and California. When Mexico was beaten by our superior arms, our might made her cede to us by treaty more than 850,000 square miles of her domain, sixteen times as much as the great State of New York.

By the same spirit we took over the Philippines without so much as asking by their leave. When the inhabitants resented our intrusion into their affairs, we sent armies and compelled them to submit. For them the consent of the governed was not considered essential. Self-determination was not accorded them. They were promised liberty when they were able to use it properly, and we claimed the right to judge the case. With us also the war god got in his work.

2. Revenge also has been a mighty appeal for the war god's use in starting strife. Speaking of the Egyptian invasion of Asia in the distant past Rawlinson ascribed it to a desire for vengeance upon a hated foe: "Provoked by an attack upon her from the side of Asia, and smarting from wounds inflicted upon her pride and prosperity by the Hyksos, Egypt set herself to retaliate;

and for three centuries she continued at intervals to pour her armies into the extensive and populous regions which lay between the Mediterranean and the Zagros mountain range." Starting out thus to punish an enemy she learned her own strength, and tasted the sweets of conquest. It was like a tiger tasting blood. She wanted more. In the name of Sutek or other of her gods of war she seized upon some of the fairest portions of the earth, and became one of the most arrogant and aggressive nations on the globe. In it all she justified her unjust course with the pretext of righting an ancient wrong.

When the Ionian Greeks undertook to cast off the b urden imposed by Cyrus the Elamite and continued by his successors in power, they naturally had the sympathy of their brethren in Attica. On hearing of the matter Darius, who had succeeded to the Persian throne, asked: "Who are these Athenians?" Having received reply he shot an arrow into the air, at the same time calling upon the god whose aid he sought: "O Zeus, grant that I may avenge myself on these Athenians." He instructed a servant to say three times at every noon-day meal: "Master, remember the Athenians." As he prepared for his expedition of plunder in Greece, his passion for conquest was strengthened by his passion for revenge, and in the name of his god he openly announced his purpose to chastise the audacious and insolent Greeks. In the matter of conquest he failed, but he gave vent to his animosity; and when he died, both his spirit and his schemes passed over to his son.

The Greeks also cherished resentment for the things which they suffered under Darius and Xerxes. Later dawned the day of their revenge. Rawlinson wrote: "It was now the turn of the Greeks to retaliate on their prostrate foe. First under the lead of Sparta and then under that of Athens they freed the islands of the Ægean from the Persian yoke, expelled the Persian garrisons from Europe, and even ravaged the Asiatic coast and made descents upon it at their pleasure." Demosthenes and his countrymen sternly resented the Macedonian dominion, but the bitterness of it was assuaged in part as later the Greeks saw Alexander treading their ancient foes beneath his ruthless feet. Their service of Ares was rendered with greater zest, because it furnished an opportunity for the vengeance which they desired to inflict.

Whatever the instigation of the first Punic war, which was forced upon a reluctant Roman Senate by vote of the people, it evoked the spirit of revenge on the part of Carthage, and caused Hamilcar to lead his son to the altar and swear him to unending hatred against the Romans. Arnold says: "It led most surely to that fearful visitation of Hannibal's sixteen years' invasion of Italy, which destroyed forever, not indeed the pride of Roman dominion, but the wellbeing of the Roman people." In turn Hannibal's invasion of Italy inflicted on Roman pride a wound that could be healed only in blood. For years Cato cried in the ears of the Senate: "*Carthago delenda est*"; and the time came when the decree of the stern old Censor was executed to the letter. Under the inspiration of Mars Carthage was basely tricked and betrayed. Another Scipio, grandson of the Africanus, fought his way street by street into the heart of the city. Under instructions from home he levelled every building to the ground, and sent the surviving inhabitants to be sold as slaves in the markets of Rome.

Through the centuries the smart of wounds inflicted in war has aroused the spirit of revenge in those who suffered, and has instigated war in return. Among the thousands of treaties that have marked the close of hostilities on the field probably not one has ever been considered just and fair by all parties concerned. Usually the victors make the terms. They have the advantage, and they seldom fail to use it for their own ends. The vanquished have to submit, but the sense of injustice remains to rankle and bite.

Lately for months men of various and contrary creeds sat in council at Versailles over a treaty of peace. They represented only the victors in the strife, who in contrast with the vanquished were more than five to one. An *ex parte* court of confessed enemies to those whom they judged, they duly found them guilty in their absence, and proceeded to pass judgment. "Whithersoever the carcase is thither will the vultures be gathered together."

With less ambition than their beaten foes they proceeded to gratify their smaller desires as they were able. England wanted territory in Asia and Africa. Belgium wanted a part of Holland. France wanted

Alsace and Lorraine and other territory belonging to the prostrate foe. Italy desired Fiume and portions of Tyrol. Servia and Rumania each coveted a part of Austria. Greece yearned for certain Turkish possessions. Japan claimed Korea, the scene of her atrocities, also Shantung with its alien population and wealth and certain islands in the Pacific.

Further to satisfy their greed they laid upon generations unborn and incapable of any responsibility in the matter a crushing burden of debt as a penalty for iniquities in which they had no part. It was not satisfactory to anybody, but it was the best our statesmanship could devise. In the end it was confessed a league for war rather than peace. The war god presided, and got in his work.

Sometimes the offense that instigates a war of revenge is so trivial as to excite contempt. Against Spain, England waged a destructive war, which is known in history as the War of Jenkins' Ear, an English ship captain having lost an ear at the hands of certain reckless subjects of the Spanish crown. Concerning the matter Morris wrote: "Walpole, always anxious for peace, by argument, by negotiation, by delays, resisted the desire for war. At last he could resist no longer. For the sake of his reputation he should have resigned his office; but he had enjoyed power too long to yield it, and he most unwisely allowed himself to be forced into a declaration of war."

It was the old story of yielding to popular clamour. For so small a cause the war god had his way, and the act was hailed with delight throughout the land.

Of course Jenkins needed his ear. It was part of his natural equipment for the business of life. It was an outrage for the unruly Spaniards to hurt and disfigure him so. But the war to avenge Jenkins' loss in no wise repaired the damage that was done. It did not restore the missing member. On the contrary, it cost not only other ears and eyes and arms and legs, but also thousands of precious lives. The war god played the game to success.

3. Liberty has served him well as a plea for war, the various applications of the term only rendering it more effective for his sinister designs. The cry of the ages has been the cry of the oppressed. Lew Wallace may tell of Ben Hur falsely accused and robbed of his estate, held in durance vile and chained to the galleys of Rome, or of defenseless women thrust into reeking dungeons to stiffen and starve amid vermin and disease; Victor Hugo may follow Jean Valjean from prison to prison, tracing through a thousand pages the pathetic career of one who sinned and suffered and was plunged into deeper sin; Charles Dickens may tax his ingenuity to portray the horrors of the Bastille and the reactionary horrors enacted by an ignorant populace stung to madness by the wrongs that they suffered, but the story of human oppression has never been told. If all that the weak have suffered at the hands of the strong could be put into words and written into books, no heart would be stout enough to read the gruesome tale. The assertion of man's right to be free and the struggle to

maintain that right constitute at once the romance and the tragedy of history.

Egypt groaned under the burdens imposed by the Hyksos, and were willing to fight for relief. In turn Israel deeply felt the oppressions of the Pharaohs: "The Egyptians made the children of Israel serve with rigour, and made their lives bitter with hard bondage in mortar and in brick and in all manner of service in the field. ... And the children of Israel sighed by reason of the bondage; they cried, and their cry came up unto God. And God heard their groanings, and he remembered his covenant; and God said, 'I have surely seen the affliction of my people who are in Egypt, and have heard their cry by reason of their taskmasters; I know their sorrows, and I have come down to deliver them out of the hand of the Egyptians, and to bring them up out of that land unto a land good and large.'" The record of the deliverance, as God guided his chosen, is one of the remarkable stories in the annals of time.

The revolt of Cyrus the Great against Astyages the king of Media, and of Ionian cities against Darius 1, and of the Greeks against Alexander, and of Babylon against Xerxes, and of Egypt against Darius Nothus, and of the Caducians and also of the Egyptians against Artaxerxes, and of Cyrus the Younger against his brother, and of Judas Maccabæus against Antiochus, and of certain provinces in Gaul and also of certain others in Asia against Julius Cæsar, and of Palestine and Silicia against Ptolemy Soter, and of Danelagh and Northumbria against William the Norman, and of Wat Tyler against Richard II, and of Owen Glendower against Henry IV, and of Joan of Arc against the Duke of Bedford, and of Jack Cade against Henry VI, and of Thomas Wyat against Bloody Mary, and of Oliver Cromwell against Charles I, and of George Washington and also of Robert Emmet against George III, and of Victor Emmanuel against Pius IX, and of Roger Casement against George V – these are some of the historic efforts to regain lost liberties through an appeal to the god of war.

The insurrection led by Nat Turner in Virginia in 1831 was the blind effort of an ignorant slave to cast off the chains that held him and to wreak vengeance on those whom he regarded as his oppressors. Like Joan of Arc, he claimed to be inspired from heaven to do his bloody work. Making humble confession of his cruel deeds he said: "On the 12th day of May, 1828, I heard a loud noise in the heavens, and the spirit instantly appeared to me, and said the serpent was loosed and Christ had laid down the yoke he had borne for the sins of men, and that I should take it on and fight against the serpent: for the time was fast approaching when the first should be last and the last first, and that by signs in the heavens it would be made known unto me when I should commence the great work." Until the sign appeared he was to tell no man the things that were in his heart.

In February, 1831, there was an eclipse of the sun. To the superstitious negro it was the sign for which he was waiting, and he interpreted it that "I should arise and prepare myself, and slay my, enemies with their own weapons. Immediately on the sign appearing in the heavens the seal was removed from my lips, and I communicated the great work laid out for me to do to four men in whom I had the greatest confidence."

Like true servants of the war god, he and others alike enslaved, possibly scarred with the lash of the taskmaster and separated from their best beloved, armed themselves with guns and swords and such other weapons as they could secure, and went forth to kill without remorse in the name of the liberty which they craved. In their ignorance and fury they spared neither age nor sex, and even little children were butchered without a pang of pity or regret."O Liberty, what crimes are committed in thy name!"

The god of war has never been able to make men free indeed , and at best he can only change the pressure of the yoke. Beyond the purpose to kill and maim and mangle he has no fixed principles, and his purpose is equally accomplished either in victory or defeat. Often he moves men to fight for liberty, and then abandons them to their fate. When Pharotes led Parthia and Hyrcania into an insurrection against the tyranny of Darius, he was caught; "his nose and ears and tongue were cut off, his eyes were torn from their sockets, and finally he was impaled." Leonidas and his three hundred stood at The Gates to defend the liberties of Sparta against the hordes of Persia, but the god of battles forsook him in his hour of need.

" 'Twas an hour of fateful issues,
When the bold three hundred stood,
For the love of freedom,
By the old Thessalian flood, –
When lifting high each sword of flame
They called on every sacred name,
And swore beside those dashing waves
They never, never would be slaves.

And, oh, that oath was nobly kept.
From morn to setting sun
Did desperation urge the fight,
Which valour had begun;
And torrent like, the stream of blood
Ran down, and mingled with the flood;
But all, from mountain cliff to wave,
Was glory's, valour's, freedom's grave."

The sacredness of the cause did not secure the aid of the war god, and only one was left to tell the tale. Gutruatus, chief of the Carnutes, who rose up against the oppressions of Cæsar in Western Gaul, was caught and taken to Cæsar's camp; he was beaten with rods until he fainted from pain and was then beheaded. In a few short months after Joan of Arc had "liberated France," as they said, and had seen her favourite duly seated on the throne, she was basely forsaken, falsely accused, unjustly condemned, and brutally burned alive by the base people whom she had served.

Through the centuries other ardent champions of liberty have met a similar fate. The desire for liberty serves the war god's unholy purpose as a means of instigating violence and bloodshed, but except in the minds of those who do such deeds it does not justify the killing of those who work oppression. And Nat Turner was caught and hanged.

> "He struck, fair Liberty, for thee;
> He died: to die is to be free."

4. Patriotism furnishes the war god an effective plea for starting war. The term is vague and variable, and it easily fits into many conditions. It is derived from the Greek *patris*, like the Latin *patria*, meaning native place or fatherland; and in popular usage it connotes the love of one's country, a very proper sentiment. But what is one's country, as the term is used in the definition? It is not the rural districts in contrast with towns and cities, nor fields and forests as distinguished from houses and streets.

With fine sentiment poets have dwelt upon the theme, but they have felt no need to define. In glowing fervour Scott exclaims:

> "Lives there a man with soul so dead,
>   Who never to himself hath said:
>   This is my own, my native land!"

"This." What? Certainly true patriotism is not confined to such as continue in the land of their nativity. Many of our highly useful and loyal citizens were born on foreign soil. There is more reason for loving the place of one's residence, which is usually a matter of choice, than for loving the place of one's birth, which is never of his own selection.

Our national poet, Samuel F. Smith, brings us the patriotic strain:

"My native country, thee,
Land of the noble free,
　　Thy name I love:
I love thy rocks and rills,
Thy woods and templed hills;
My heart with rapture thrills,
　　Like that above."

And here it is still a matter of nativity; no place for patriotism on the part of such as are not native, and no reason assigned or suggested why rocks and rills, woods and hills on the right bank of the Saint Lawrence or the left bank of the Rio Grande should be considered more beautiful and thrilling than similar objects just across those streams, the same God above being the Maker of them all and equally interested in them all.

Looking across from the bloody fields of France another poet defines the object of his patriotic fervour in these simple words:

"Not power most of all,
Nor even liberty,
Nor wealth, nor fame,
Nor honour brightly kept,
Nor the high title of democracy, –
    Of refuge, haven,
    The land of equal chance;

But simply this to me:
The little house beneath the elms,
    Where I was born,
    And played on brittle days
    At soldier with my dog.

Just these simple things,
That go to make my home .
    And how I love you!"

Another earnest writer includes these things in his definition, but goes farther: "This primal love of the earth which has borne you and your ancestors seems to be stronger, more passionate, with the Europeans than with the Americans. Even for the peasant lad joining the colours to fight for his country patriotism is something more complex than love of the soil. It is love of life as he has known it, its language, its customs, its aspects, the mother he has known, the men and women of his race, and deeper yet the history that has made him and his what they are, and the ideals that have been committed to them for the coming generations.

It is the better part of man woven into the tissue of his being."

Some have adopted the terms of social science in the effort to make their meaning clear, and have spoken of the group consciousness, whatever that is, as the heart of patriotism. Others make the government under which one lives the expression of the country's life and the centre of the citizen's devotion. In the case of Germany President Wilson tried to make a distinction between the government and the people, frequently asserting that he was proposing to fight the first, but not the last. In the end the distinction failed; and after the government was overthrown and the rulers sent into exile, the people were penalized for the acts of the government which they had repudiated.

As popularly conceived the stable element in patriotism is simply a state of mind, while in its objective element it is essentially provincial. Touching these points Mr. Roosevelt, who wore a military title, says: "The pale conception of internationalism and human brotherhood, whether a class interest of the worker or an intellectual ideal of a dreamer, cannot stand before the passion of patriotism."

He further uses these contemptuous words of such as have come into the larger conception of human brotherhood: "Those beings who become citizens of the world, wandering physically and intellectually from land to land, our cosmopolites and intellectuals, froth of too easy existence, give forth a hollow sound at the touch of war. They become pacifists."

It is a remarkable thing, that under the domination of the war god the man who loves his country too well to want her plunged into the maelstrom of war is not considered a patriot. John Bright rises in the British House of Commons to say: "Even if I were alone, if mine were the solitary voice raised amid the din of arms and the clamour of a venal press, I should have the priceless consolation that no word of mine has tended to produce the squandering of a penny of my country's treasure and the spilling of a drop of my country's blood;" but he is giving forth a hollow sound. He is a cosmopolite, a pacifist, a servant of the God of Peace, who loved the world rather than any particular province or locality.

Remarkable also are the contradictions which patriotism engenders in the interest of war. For example, Abraham Lincoln and U. S. Grant, Jefferson Davis and R. E. Lee were born in the same country and under the same flag. Lincoln and Grant were accounted patriots for planning and fighting to preserve the country and uphold the flag, while Davis and Lee were accounted patriots for planning and fighting to disrupt the country, and put down the flag in certain States. Also eastern counties of Virginia were patriotic in seceding from the Union, and western counties were equally patriotic in refusing to secede, preferring rather to secede from the old State. And as ever the war god used that patriotism for his sinister purposes.

The same sort of patriotism moves the Hun, the Jap, the Prussian, the Turk, the savage of any degree to fight.

Macaulay represents the pagan Roman as glowing with patriotic fervour as he fought the invading hosts of Lars Porsena:

> "And how can man die better
>> Than in facing fearful odds,
> For the ashes of his fathers,
>> And the temples of his gods?"

By this standard the modern Teutons prove themselves patriots of high degree, saying: "We love our Fatherland so much that we gladly barter our heavenly for it." Such an utterance recalls the definition given by Samuel Johnson, the English lexicographer of the eighteenth century: "Patriotism is the last refuge of a scoundrel."

5. Religion also serves the war god's purposes. It is any form of divine faith and worship. It touches the deep things in human experience. The war god knows its power, and has used it in various forms for arousing men to butcher one another.

The famous siege and sacking of Troy engaged the chief gods of the pantheon. Called by their Latin names, Neptune favoured the Greeks, and Juno and Minerva sided with him, the female of the species being as deadly as the male. Mars and Venus opposed, the beautiful Apollo veered from side to side, while the great Jupiter looked on with varying degrees of interest. The Greeks won, the gods approving the ruses of war, as does also the modern Hague.

Six hundred years before Christ Ares moved Athens to undertake what was called a sacred war. On the bay of Corinth lived a brave and lawless tribe that coveted the treasures stored in the temple of Apollo at Delphi; and fearing neither god nor man they besieged the place and took possession. Solon gathered the Athenian assembly, cited the sacrilege, and urged the people to take up arms in defense of the god, who seemed in a poor way. After about ten years of war the Athenians won, the god was duly vindicated, and the Pythian games celebrated the famous victory.

Later Ares incited Thebes and Phocis to a religious war, which lasted several years. In some way the Phocians as judged by the Thebans failed in their religious duties; the Theban council brought a charge of sacrilege against their neighbours, and imposed a heavy fine. With amazing valour the Phocians resisted the imposition. They seized the city, and destroyed the records of the council that had passed judgment against them. They also appropriated the vast treasures that were stored in the temple, and used them for advancing their own cause.

When Philip of Macedon sought a pretext for invading Grecian territory, it was ready furnished. He marched forward with the avowed purpose of rescuing the temple from the desecrating robbers. Athens and Sparta were drawn into the conflict, and after six years of butchery and blood Delphi was duly rescued, Phocis was properly punished, the sacred war was at an end, but Greece was under the heel of Philip.

Paganism is not the only religion that lends itself to the schemes of the war god. The Allah of Mohammed was essentially god of battles. The prophet was by nature man kind and gentle spirit, as his deeds abundantly show; only the service of his god was he stern and relentless. In the early days of his career there was no hint of the sword means of extending the faith; but he saw men closing their eyes the light and resisting the evidence of his miracles, and he heard a voice urging him sterner means. In obedience to the word which came to him he said: "The sword is the key heaven and hell; a drop of blood shed the cause of god, a night spent in arms, is of more avail than two months of fasting and prayer."

Religious enthusiasm enhanced the passion for military exploits, and the two together burned in the souls of the faithful with flame which nothing could quench. The battles waged were more than Homeric in the reckless abandon and ruthless cruelty which they displayed. One young hero who feared that he might be rejected by the prophet on account of tender age dissembled, and secured a place in the ranks; he then cast away his food and plunged into the fray, declaring that when next he ate it would be in the presence of his god. At Yermuk the faithful were urged to fight by the assurance that Paradise was before them, and the devil and hell fire in the rear, and they were exhorted to persevere until there was no temptation to idolatry and religion became god's alone; and so encouraged they courted death with the ecstasy of martyrs anticipating a crown of glory just beyond. At Aiznadin a single soldier attacked a squad of thirty men, and killed seventeen before he fell. At Damascus a Saracen woman who had followed her husband in the holy war saw him killed; she stopped just long enough to bury him, and then taking up her weapons she fought until she had slain the archer who shot her husband. With every Mussulman it was Allah's battle, and as his god willed he was ready for victory or for death.

The war god has also used various corrupted forms of Christianity to kindle strife and spill blood. Forgetting that spiritual weapons under the power of God are mighty enough to overthrow every stronghold of Satan and bring complete conquest, some who have assumed the Christian name have resorted to carnal weapons and physical force in a vain effort to dethrone evil and establish righteousness in the earth.

When Constantine found himself opposed by other claimants to the throne of the Roman empire, he perceived that it would enhance his prospects to have the support of the Christians of the realm, who had grown both numerous and powerful. As if to suggest something analogous to the conversion of Saul of Tarsus, he said that at midday he saw in the heavens a flaming cross, shining above the brightness of the sun and bearing in letters Greek the words, "Conquer by This." He further said that with the coming of night he fell asleep, and saw in a vision the Christ approaching him with the same sign, and commanding him to place it upon his standards and carry it as a safeguard against all enemies. He professed conversion, though in his subsequent life he did not bring forth fruits meet for repentance. From that time he adopted the labarum, called the standard of the cross, for his armies; he had the shields of his soldiers embossed with the Greek letter Chi, the initial of the name of Christ, and repudiating the Sword of the Spirit as a sufficient weapon of conquest he went in the spirit of coercion and violence to make Christians of Pagans. How thoroughly he subverted the spirit of Christianity, let the centuries of hatred and suspicion and bloodshed in Europe attest.

Wars of Charles Martel, waged against both Pagans and Mohammedans, and the wars of Charlemagne, and the Crusades which incarnadined three continents, and the religious wars of France lasting almost a hundred years, and the thirty years' war waged with desolating fury, and many other disastrous conflicts were instigated by the god of war through an appeal to the religious sentiments of men. In the great war whose echoes are still reverberating round the globe every nation engaged tried to put religion of some sort back of its deadly work.

6. In contrast with freedom slavery sometimes furnishes the war god an effective plea. All wars of conquest are based on avarice, and slavery as a source of wealth has often been a result of victory. Among the early Greeks the right of might established the custom of enslaving such prisoners taken in war as were not

ransomed or killed; and sometimes they were women of beauty and men of renown, sold in the markets for such prices as they would bring. In such cases slavery was an incident of war rather than its chief purpose.

Pharaoh's pursuit of escaping Israel was probably the earliest recorded instance of armies making an attack in the avowed interest of human slavery. Centuries later the English South Sea Company made marauding expeditions into Africa for the purpose of capturing natives for slaves, but the attacks were considered commercial enterprises rather than military exploits.

Early in the sixteenth century slaves and sugar culture were introduced into Cuba. That event coupled with the fact that the Spanish government felt constrained to issue an order forbidding the enslavement of the natives suggests that Hernando de Soto set out from Havana to invade Florida with the idea of bringing Indians into slavery. Certainly he made them burden bearers in his explorations of the Southwest.

In 1836 Texas seceded from the Republic of Mexico, the latter having previously abolished slavery in all her territory. Santa Anna resisted the disruption of the country, and marched with an army to put down the secession movement, committing atrocities along the way and butchering prisoners both at Alamo and Goliad. He was met and defeated at San Jacinto, and the Texas war for slavery was a success.

The same spirit caused the aggressions which led to our war with Mexico in 1846, and to the seizure of Mexican territory at its close. Later it inspired the attack on Fort Sumter, and caused the fratricidal war that followed. A war for slavery may be as bloody as any, and quite as pleasing to the wicked god that inspires men to kill and destroy one another.

7. The war god is adroit enough to use peace also as an effective plea for his bloody work. Such a plea reverses the primal laws of thought, and taxes confidence in the reliability of human understanding; but for centuries it has been put forward by men who seemed to believe what they said. More than a thousand years ago Pepin the Short, a sort of German Quilp, put forth the plea. The historian says he continued his never-ending wars in Germany and Gaul with the avowed object of securing peace by the sword; at the same time he trained his son and successor to continue the fighting with more bitterness and brutality than he himself had shown. His modern Teuton successors have taken up the cry, and have seriously declared that in the bloodiest of all wars they were fighting for enduring peace.

Others have been dominated by the German mind, and have fallen into the same folly. Lord Balfour said every British and French soldier would leave the trenches in twenty-four hours, if he did not believe that he was fighting to kill war. The Padre who wrote "Rough Rhymes" put these touching words into the mouth of a simple soldier who was facing death in utter bewilderment as to what it was all about:

"Gawd knows I ain't no thinker,
    And I never was before,
But I know now why I'm fighting:
    It's to put an end to war."

In finer tone a current poem sets the thought in these words:

"We stand in the way of the war god,
    Where the little streams run red;
We have sworn we will kill the war god,
    And will die for the word we said.
We swear that the fields shall be green again,
    And the children shall have bread."

The German drive in the spring of 1918 was called a peace offensive, and the popular talk for a time was talk of fighting for peace.

Sometimes the sons of a drunken father have been so humiliated by the family poverty and disgrace that they have forsworn forever the use of strong drink; but so far as is known no drunkard ever openly announced that he was indulging his base appetite and debauching himself in the interest of sobriety. Many have been the idolatries that have debased the sons of men; but there is no record that the sons of Belial ever professed to be acting in the interest of the first and second commandments. The name of God has often been blasphemed and the Sabbath desecrated; but the sinners have not usually professed to be sinning in order to sanctify the law.

In the days of Christ there were some who by a jugglery of words undertook to evade the commandment which bound them to honour and support their fathers and mothers, and Jesus blasted them with a single utterance: "Hypocrites, ye make void the word of God!"

Uncleanness and theft, lying and covetousness have existed in some measure in all ages and nations; but the men who have transgressed the law have never claimed that they were sinning in the interest of chastity and virtue, honesty and truth. If for a moment they were to offer such a plea for their wickedness, they would be laughed to scorn. But the war god so warps the minds of men that they trample the law under foot, and go forth hating men and working desolation and death, and are yet able to look the world in the face and say they are doing their dreadful work in the interest of life and peace. Sometimes the men who make the shallow pretense are hailed as statesmen and philosophers, though they urge preparation for larger war while they talk of permanent peace.

V

Temples and Sacrifices

God who abides in the high and holy place, creating worlds and systems of worlds, dwells not in temples made with hands. Thus said he to David: "Thou shalt not build me a house to dwell in. For I have not dwelt in a house since the day that I brought up Israel unto this day, but I have gone from tent to tent and from a tabernacle. Wheresoever I have walked with Israel have I spoken with any of the Judges whom I commanded to shepherd my people, saying, Why have ye not built me a house of cedars?"

When at last the temple was built, it became a symbol of the spiritual abode fixed for God in the hearts of men. When it became a sacred object to draw the devotions of devout hearts to itself, it was thrown down, not one stone being left upon another. In all the New Testament there is no mention of any Christian house of worship of any kind; rather the people themselves are mentioned as God's culture, God's building, a spiritual house, a holy priesthood, to offer up spiritual sacrifices acceptable to God through Jesus Christ.

In contrast with this simplicity and spirituality, heathenism in all its forms has always appealed to the spectacular and sensuous. From times remote the god of war has instigated the erection of massive and ornate temples in his honour. In old Shushan where Xerxes held his court and worked his abominations, the house of Asshur was like a palace in magnificence. It was the chief architectural attraction of the city, and was called the House of the Great Mountain of the Land. There the war god was worshipped with elaborate rites and votive offerings, and the spirit of cruelty and conquest was kept alive in the hearts of the people.

The House of Marduk was open for all in Babylon. By appropriate forms and ceremonies the spirit of pride and oppression was kept aglow. In the fury of that spirit weaker peoples were trampled down and brought into subjection, and Marduk's power was extended to the Mediterranean and the Nile.

In dim and enormous temples in Memphis and Thebes Sutek gathered his worshippers and received their offerings. He imparted his spirit to his devotees, and the Egyptians became proud and pitiless and scornful, willing always to measure right by the rule of might.

Greek cities famous for architecture did not fail to provide for Ares. In Olympia and Sparta he was duly housed. In Athens his temple was one of the notable structures of the city. It stood in stately grandeur on an eminence called the Areopagus, or Hill of Ares, and was one of an aggregation of buildings dedicated to national glory and known throughout the world. In its solemn courts Ares was honoured with pomp and circumstance, the spirit of envy and hatred was duly fostered and the inevitable results ensued.

Athens and Sparta and other cities of Hellas, peopled by a common stock and having common interests, gathered their armies from time to time to kill and destroy one another. The historic Peloponnesian war, involving the chief cities of Greece, was waged with a fury and destructiveness limited only by the capacity of those engaged. It was Greek against Greek, brother against brother in deadly conflict; and all were controlled by the same spirit, the spirit nurtured in the temples of Ares.

In Rome there were several temples to Mars. The greatest of them was built on the Campus Martius. It stood as a silent symbol of the divine presence. It indicated the pleasure of the war god in the savagery and suffering inflicted by war, and it impressed the Roman soldier with the dignity and holiness of his calling. In its solemn shadows men were drilled for the ruthless service which they had assumed, and with the implied approval of the war god they became the fearless fighters known in history.

Another structure less renowned was erected just without the city wall. It stood by the Porta Capena, which opened on the Appian Way, which the stately columns took as they marched forth under the eye of the god to meet and vanquish their foes.

Like the gods of the Amorites, the Perizzites and other ancient peoples, Odin was worshipped in the temples of the forest. The old Teutons looked to the rugged scenes of nature for suitable places to worship the rugged god of war. In the shadows of gnarled trees whose knotted branches indicated fierce fighting with many a storm, they bowed before the god of battles and implored his aid in the barbarous work they loved so well.

Nations that do not openly allow the existence of such a god have nevertheless made ample provision for his service. Contrary to the expressed will of God that nations shall not learn war any more, they have conceived and established institutions for the avowed purpose of diverting young men from the paths of peace, filling them with the spirit of class and caste, obliterating the idea of equality and brotherhood, teaching them to dominate their fellow-men and to lead them out to waste their lives in camps and barracks or perchance to destroy themselves in the effort to destroy others. For the foul purposes of the war god such buildings are more effective than the finest temples ever erected by Grecian skill.

Supplemental to these there are in the chief cities of Europe and America other notable structures erected at public expense and maintained from the same source, which are devoted to the purpose of training in the rules and customs of war such young men as have not had the advantages of the technical schools, and preparing them especially for the lower ranks of those who serve the fateful god. Not in name, to be sure, but in fact all such buildings are the natural successors of the ancient war god temples, and they accomplish his work in a better way.

Temples and altars and the god who presides over

them invariably demand sacrifices. By intuition or by instruction that was recorded only in after times Cain and Abel brought their respective offerings unto God. Later it was said: "Speak unto the children of Israel, that they bring me an offering."

According to the law offerings of various kinds were required of the people, classified according to the manner of the making or the purpose for which they were made. Casual reading may suggest a great drain upon the resources of the worshippers, but closer study shows that the waste was comparatively small. There were whole burnt offerings for sin, but they were an inconsiderable part of the Mosaic ritual. The blood of countless beasts was shed, but it was not an article of food; often the flesh of the animals sacrificed was put to useful purposes. Many other offerings were simply heaved or waved before the Lord, and then used in the service of his people. The true God demanded the best, but demanded it only to make it more effective in the service of man. For himself he needed nothing.

On the contrary, the god of war has no concern for the welfare of his subjects. Like the daughters of the horse-leech, he forever cries, "Give, give." His demands extend to every form of material wealth and every treasure of sacred sentiment, and they are insatiable. In the end the sacrifices which he requires represent absolute and irreparable waste.

Least in intrinsic worth are the material sacrifices which he demands. "Who steals my purse steals trash." Yet the sum of this sort of trash demanded by the god of war is frankly amazing. From the earliest times the war god has been making his demands upon the resources of the race, but the ancient records were not preserved. What it cost Nebuchadnezzar to transport troops from the Euphrates to the Nile, or what it cost Xerxes to invade Greece, can never be known. The campaigns of Cyrus and Alexander, Hannibal and Cæsar were conducted at vast expense, but not even a rough estimate of it all has been preserved. Other wars of ancient times consumed uncounted treasure, and left the masses of the people to stagger under the burden of poverty and debt.

There was also immense indirect loss. Men were drawn away from productive pursuits, each withdrawal causing a decrease in productive energy. In the matter of food and raiment, arms and ammunition, the upkeep of the armies was an additional tax on those left to produce. Cities were burned and fields desolated, sheep and cattle driven away and all forms of labour disorganized. Desolation followed every army, whether in victory or defeat.

In historic times the material cost of serving the war god has not been accurately kept, but the meagre records that have been preserved show a loss beyond the power of man to comprehend. In 1913 the bonded debts of the cities and nations of the civilized world, as computed by David Starr Jordan, reached the staggering sum of sixty thousand millions of dollars or more. Directly or indirectly the larger part of this intolerable burden is traceable to the service of the war god, and yet he piles the load higher and higher every day. Before the crime of 1914 the interest on the world's war debt was computed at a thousand millions a year.

To this was added the burden of thousands of millions more to maintain vast armies even in times of peace. The remarkable apology offered for the burdensome outlay was that it was made in the interest of peace, preparation for breaking the peace being the best means to secure that end. In our own land according to the spirit of the comment we boast or complain that when the recent storm broke over us we were quite unprepared for the event; and yet for the last fifty years about two-thirds of the nation's revenues were expended in connection with war. Two for war to one for peace, and yet unprepared, so greedy are the demands of the war god. How our country would bloom and blossom as the rose, if half the sum could be devoted to the public works of peace!

In our Civil War, according to a statement by ex-Governor Hanly, the actual money expense of the two governments was sixteen thousand millions of dollars. This was four thousand for every negro liberated, half the sum being twice the price of a good slave. We came to a time when our problems were bigger than our statesmanship. Under stress of inflamed passions we lost our composure; we bowed to the will of the war god, and took up the law of the jungle. From the treasure gathered by years of toil we madly poured out four times as much as all the slaves in the land were worth if sold on the market. In the end the negroes, worth as a financial asset some four thousand millions more, were a total loss, and without the slightest show of justice it was made to fall especially upon the citizens who happened to hold that form of property.

It has been quite widely urged, and quite widely believed, that we as Americans were forced into the big world war. It is a confession that at some point we were whipped, brought into subjection to some superior force that we could not resist, and made to do what we did not want to do. The power that forced us was the power of the war god, the same that coerced the Teutons. When he got us, he worked us. According to the late Senator Martin we voted for the service in about eighteen months the staggering sum of fifty-seven thousand millions of dollars, and were ready to vote as much more. It was a tribute such as no tyrant ever exacted of a fallen foe; and we gave it gladly, and were ready to brand as an alien and an enemy any citizen who doubted the wisdom of such a tax.

Other nations were equally responsive to the demands of the war god. Bismarck was called the Iron Chancellor. He was accounted the foe of France. In 1871 he laid a tax of a thousand million dollars on the French people, and sent them home to make the money; in 1914 and the three years immediately following the rulers of France, claiming to be friends and lovers, levied more than ten times as much on the same people, and sent the men out to kill and get killed by machinery. Their enemies were equally devoted to the war god, and the inevitable result was desolation wide and irreparable.

Premier Clemenceau, who resented the first experience and approved the second, stated the case in part in these pathetic words: "The industrial life of France has been so wrecked that its resuscitation is most difficult, while by reason of her military surrender (rejecting the war god) Germany has been able to save her industries intact and ready for immediate and efficient operation. Industrially and commercially, as between France and Prussia, for the present the victory is with the Hun. And financially, by reason of the blockade, the value of which as a military factor no one will question, the German war debt is almost wholly a debt to her own people, easily repudiated, while the debt of France is one which must be paid. Here again the war has proven something like a Pyrrhic victory for France.

"The French fortune invested abroad before the war was large, some fifty billion or sixty billion francs of French stocks. What has become of that fortune? The best we can hope for is that payments on about two-thirds of it may be considered as simply deferred; that the immense sum accumulated by French thrift and loaned abroad will be collected eventually.

"France has something like twenty billion francs invested in Russia, two-thirds of that sum in Russian government securities and the remainder in industrial enterprises. The French people had other billions in

Balkan and Turkish obligations. Then just before the war the disorders in Mexico deprived us of the revenue from about two and a half billion francs invested there, and we are having the same experience with several other billions in South America, notably in the immense French investments in railroads."

This is an official statement of the blight which the service of the war god put upon France in what was called a glorious victory, but it is not all. The Premier proceeds to say: "The paying investments abroad are relatively inconsiderable compared with the debts which France has contracted abroad during the war, especially in America and in England. ... If our national debts were only due to our own people, the problem would not be so difficult, because we would not have to consider the sending out of the country of great sums at disadvantageous rates of exchange. The money from the French people for interest on the national debt would be distributed among French people, unequally perhaps, but nevertheless the interest would remain in the country to be used partly for reconstruction and as capital for the development of industrial life."

In other lands the recent tribute to the war god has been on a similar scale. Every nation that has bowed the knee to him has been the loser, and the aggregate cost in money has been put at two hundred thousand millions of dollars and more.

In its final use this vast wealth has been in the nature of a burnt offering, but has brought no atonement. Powder burnt, gases loosed, shells exploded, missiles thrown away, vehicles worn out, ships sunk or outclassed, camps abandoned, materials used up, food devoured to sustain armies that accomplish nothing when not fighting and only desolation when engaged. The talk about reparation is partly ignorance, partly hypocrisy, partly nonsense. After the fiercest storm something is left. After a fire there are the ashes and the lot on which the building stood. After the flood Noah and his household may go forth to repeople the desolate earth, but they cannot restore the things that have been swept away. After the desolations of war the remnants of the race, cripples and widows and orphans, may take up the struggle and strive to restore the wreckage, but they can never retrieve the tribute which the war god has exacted. Some good survives every war, but it is a different proposition to show that any good not better achieved by ways of peace has ever resulted from war.

And the burden bears heaviest on those least able to endure it. Sometimes great corporations charge up their war tax to the goods they sell. In war rich men have surplus and unmissed millions to give away. Dr. J. L. M. Curry says: "It is a fact easily verified by budgets and tax bills that war taxes fall most heavily and oppressively on those least able to pay them. Articles of daily consumption, necessaries of life such as the toiling multitudes use are directly or under deceptive disguises made to pay an undue proportion of the taxes. The means of subsistence of the poor are reduced to meet government wants and to relieve those more able to contribute to the support of the government."

More than any sacrifice of material wealth is the sacrifice of principles, which the war god demands. Treaties and constitutions, public documents and religious creeds contain nothing that is sacred to the war god. He demands, and the subservient people accord with alacrity and gladness. They even account as an enemy and a slacker such as question the wisdom of such sacrifices. A few examples will illustrate what is meant.

Years ago the stronger nations of Europe entered into a solemn treaty guaranteeing Belgium's neutrality and her immunity from invasion by any of their armies. What became of the solemn compact, when Germany invaded Belgium in 1914?

The nations joined in certain formal pacts which bound belligerents in time of war to respect the rights of neutrals on the high seas and to protect the property and lives of non-combatants. What became of the pacts, when ships of neutrals were sunk and women and children were robbed and slain?

Through their official representatives duly assembled England and France and Russia drew Italy into alliance by a sacred promise, which was publicly proclaimed, not to accept any terms of peace with the central powers which were not acceptable to Italy. What became of the sacred promise, when Fiume was disposed of in a way displeasing to the Italian representatives in the peace conference?

Our Constitution clearly declares that Congress shall pass no law prohibiting the free exercise of religion, nor any law limiting freedom of speech or freedom of the press. What became of this constitutional guarantee, when an official order went forth prohibiting certain accredited ministers from preaching to their own people in the camps, and when the espionage law was passed, limiting both freedom of speech and freedom of the press, the same being recommended and passed by men doubly sworn to uphold the Constitution of the United States?

Our Declaration of Independence, which lies at the foundation of all our greatness, sets forth our faith that all men are endowed by the Creator with an inalienable right to liberty and the pursuit of happiness. What became of this sacred document, when at the instigation of an official in war service a draft act was passed, which arbitrarily exempted the man of thirty-one, and arbitrarily seized the younger man, alienated his inalienable right to liberty and the pursuit of happiness, forced him from his home and his business, stripped him of his raiment and put on him other clothes, set him under authority rank under rank and at the bottom put him under a pack as a beast of burden, fed him from public supplies, paid him a wage dictated entirely by those who alienated his rights, and sent him away from his native shores to pursue a foreign foe?

The same Declaration asserts that all men are endowed by the Creator with an inalienable right to life. In harmony with this righteous utterance our Constitution provides that no man shall be deprived of life without due process of law. If the enforcement of the draft act is sufficient process of law to justify depriving a man of life, there is no essential difference between a conscript and a convict, as Champ Clark suggested; if it is not, what becomes of the assertion of the Declaration and the guarantee of the Constitution, when a man who has been deprived of his liberty is commanded by a military over-lord to expose himself to the fire of machine guns, and is deprived of his life?

In the matter of taxation our Constitution expressly limits the power of Congress to the laying and collecting of "taxes, duties, imposts and excises to pay the debts, and to provide for the common defense and general welfare of the United States." What becomes of this constitutional limitation, when Congress levies and collects from a burdened and loyal people taxes in the sum of billions of dollars to lend to foreign governments?

The doctrine of separation between church and state is deeply written in the creed of many who profess the Christian faith. It marks a cardinal distinction between Catholics and Protestants. It is claimed by some as a special tenet. What becomes of the doctrine, when people who profess it ask and accept commissions to preach under government control and for government pay?

The Scriptures of the New Testament forbid violence and impose the duty of love and kindness even to enemies who persecute and destroy. What becomes of these Scriptures, when Christian bodies formally commit themselves to the work of wounding and killing their enemies by all the devices of modern warfare?

The answer to these questions is the same in every case. It is given in the contemptuous words of Theobald von Bethman-Hollweg. These treaties, pacts, covenants, declarations, documents, constitutions, creeds, Scriptures each and every one becomes a mere scrap of paper. On all lips, whether German, French, English, American, the justification of the sacrifice is the same: *Dies ist der Krieg, C'est la guerre,* This is war. The god of war demands it, and the court of public opinion awards it.

He does not stop with the demand of money and principle; he also asks for the holiest sentiments of the human heart. In the Letter to Romans the Apostle Paul brings an inerrable indictment against the heathen. He sets it in terms that seem to hiss with the flames of divine wrath. He makes it appear that when God has given a people up to vile affections, and given them over to a reprobate mind, to follow their own base instincts and gorge themselves with all unrighteousness, they approach the culmination of depravity as they become "covenant breakers," and reach the limit as they kill the finer sentiments of the soul and are left "without natural affection."

A hen gathers her chickens under her wings. A tigress that tears living flesh and laps warm blood has natural affection. A hyena that digs into graves and desecrates the cold forms of the dead holds fast to her offspring, and does not willingly give them up to the spoiler. Natural affection forbids the sacrifice. But the power of the war god blights natural affection, and causes men to sink down to a depth that dumb creatures have never reached, where they are glad to offer their children in sacrifice to the god of war.

Touching such a sacrifice the law spoke with great clearness: "Whosoever of the children of Israel or of the strangers that sojourn in Israel that giveth his seed unto Molech, he shall surely be put to death; the people shall stone him with stones. And I will set my face against that man, and will cut him off from among his people," saith the Lord.

In the face of such warning the people yielded, and offered up their sons in sacrifice. They lacked natural affection: "Therefore the Lord rejected all the seed of Israel, and afflicted them, and delivered them into the hand of the spoilers, until he had cast them out of his sight."

Similar degeneracy was observed in ancient Sparta. Ares was the chief divinity of the realm, and Spartan courage became proverbial. In all her history Sparta produced no great poet, nor orator, nor statesman, nor philosopher, nor sculptor, nor painter, nor architect. Her fame rested on her narrow patriotism, which did not consider Hellas large enough for two considerable cities and was bitterly jealous of Athens. Lacking in natural affection her women were especially heroic. Devoted servants of Ares mothers gladly equipped their sons for battle, buckled on their armour, and hurried them forth to kill and to be killed. The war god demanded it, and heathen women ignorant of the God of love and of peace joyfully met the cruel demand.

In recent times other mothers who have had better opportunities have shown the same cruel spirit. A poor German mother hardly knowing the meaning of her words said: "I have given both my sons to die for the Fatherland; it is my chief glory." An Alsatian mother spoke of the death of her only son with tearless complacency, and said it was an honour to him and the family. In a voice resonant with resolution a French mother who had lost four sons said: "I would gladly give the other two, if necessary." Another with some claim to culture said: "It is with a proud and broken heart that I announce the death of my beloved Alain on the field of honour." An Australian mother said: "I have lost five sons in the war; I feel the pain, and also the honour." An American mother said: "I have given two sons, and am only sorry I have not two more to give."

These women represent opposite sides in the conflict to which they refer, but they utter the same sentiment. They all equally love their sons, but they love the service of the Molech of war yet more. From heathen Peloponnesus of old down to modern times and to Christian lands, the spirit is the same. The grim god of war demands the sacrifice of the natural affection that glows in a mother's breast, and under the spell tender women of all lands are

Happy to give their darling sons
To feed the hunger of the guns.

A show of reluctance is sometimes considered a misdemeanour, if not a crime; and mothers who weep for their irreparable losses are coldly condemned as unpatriotic, while those who are more destitute of natural affection are honoured and praised.

The service also requires formal sacrifices of blood. Formerly horses and cattle were considered acceptable, and they were offered up with due ceremony. The nobler offerings were human sacrifices. These were often prisoners taken in battle. When they could not be profitably sold as slaves, it was an easy way to dispose of them. It saved keep and care, and prevented escape or trickery. The usual mode of sacrifice was by crucifixion, the barbarity of the method being especially pleasing to the god in whose honour they were slain. The ceremonial was generally enacted with exciting festivity and elaborate display.

In any case, the service requires the sacrifice of human comfort and decency. In the recent maelstrom of butchery and blood more was done for the personal comfort of soldiers than ever before. There were better facilities for transportation, better camping arrangements, better sanitation, better food, better clothing, better protection against disease, better hospitals. Agencies for comfort and relief were numerous and faithful, and they were active in every afflicted land. But with all their efforts they did not obliterate the drudgery, the sleeplessness, the weariness, the suffering originating in heat and cold, wind and rain, nor did they remove the abomination of mud and dust, filth and stench, rats and lice , and the gnawing aches and pains which such conditions inevitably impose. Even the brave heart of Donald Hankey fails under such conditions, and Mr. H. G. Wells is constrained to say: "I have never imagined a quarter of its boredom, its futility, its desolation. It is a gigantic, dusty, muddy, weedy, bloody silliness."

Along with all these sacrifices is the necessary sacrifice of life itself. The history of ancient wars does not record the numbers killed in battle. In the twelfth century Frederick I, of Germany, whom the Italians surnamed Barbarosa, had one great army almost extinguished by sunstroke. Later he gathered another great army, and invaded Italy; he stormed the city of Rome and took possession, but suddenly the entire army with hardly an exception was smitten with a deadly pestilence, and the barbarous Frederick saw the victory so dearly won melt away before the resistless march of disease.

In the historic Thirty Years' War pestilence destroyed more men than the sword destroyed. After the Protestant armies had fought their way from Sweden to the very gates of Vienna, the Bubonic plague seized upon them and decimated and destroyed them, and they were obliged to retire toward their own country. In other divisions of the army typhus fever swept down thousands. In the thirty greater engagements of that war the casualties have been estimated at fifteen per cent for the victors and thirty for the vanquished, but the same authority says these losses were inconsiderable in comparison with the numbers killed by disease.

At that time the sick received no medical attention in the army; they were left along the way to be cared for by the citizens, and they spread the disease with deadly effect. One writer records that the population of Württemberg lost three hundred thousand in five years. He also states that in the province of Saxony nine hundred thousand citizens died of disease brought in by the soldiers, and that about three-fourths of the population in the territory over which the armies swept was blotted out. It was a notable sacrifice to the god of war.

In the fifteenth century Charles the Bold assigned physicians and surgeons for troops as well as for officers, but the practice did not become general or permanent till a later time. The war god makes pestilence his ally, but he is willing for soldiers to be preserved as a means of death to others. Sometimes he destroys under the guise of saving. According to the testimony of Sir John Pringle, the army hospitals of the eighteenth century were often overrun with vermin, and were filthy beyond words. In such condition they became plague spots, and in the decade from 1731 to 1741 they carried off more than were killed in battle.

In the wars of the Spanish succession and in the seven years' war typhus fever raged as an epidemic. It passed from the soldiers to the citizens. Both in the armies and among the citizens it killed uncounted thousands.

Among students of the theme it is generally agreed that Napoleon reached the limit of indifference in regard to the sick and wounded among his men. The rule of action toward such unfortunates was abandonment. Sometimes they were huddled together in any sort of available buildings, and left to die. His chief disasters came through pestilence rather than battle. In the disastrous retreat from Moscow disease did its dreadful work. Lemazurier says the great majority of the thirty thousand French prisoners left at Vilna died of plague and pestilence.

One writer claims that all who fell into Russian hands became victims of typhus fever. Another says: "The few unfortunate soldiers who had survived the awful miseries of the march, hungry, with clothes in rags and shoes in holes, alive with vermin, with frozen and gangrened limbs, scattered in all directions, some going home and others to strongholds still in the hands of the French. Thus typhus fever which infected all parts of the army was spread in a short time over a large part of Germany. The pursuing Russians did not escape the scourge, and in the last three months of the year they lost sixty-two thousand men."

It is computed that the civilian loss from typhus fever spread among the citizens by the soldiers after the Russian campaign was more than two millions. It was an added tribute to the demands of the war god.

The campaign against Spain cost the French three

hundred thousand killed by pestilence to ninety thousand killed in battle. In 1810 and 1811 yellow fever swept over southern Spain, killing thousands of all ages and classes. In the siege of Saragossa, for example, a city of a hundred thousand citizens and thirty thousand soldiers, sixty thousand of the two classes died of the plague.

The tale is too gruesome to be prolonged. The herding of men together in the service of the war god inevitably produces filth and foulness and all the conditions that induce pestilence. The conditions furnished, the pestilence follows. In no other service would such conditions be tolerated even for beasts.

Witness the Bubonic plague mowing down the armies on either side in the Thirty Years' War, and also devastating the forces of Russia and Austria alike in the middle of the eighteenth century. Consider the ravages of typhus and typhoid, as they have marched with the various armies that have swept over Europe in past years. Recall the victims of dysentery in the armies that fought each other in our Civil War. And the cholera and the smallpox in the Crimean War, devastating the armies and sweeping out into the civilian population and working ruin vaster in proportion than that of the historic London plague. And the meningitis in our recent training camps, for whose sanitation earnest care and unlimited money were expended. More than the mysterious influenza which appeared the armies of Europe and silently spread over the whole earth taking toll of more than twelve million souls. And the deadly diseases that are now killing off the guards left to police Siberia meagrely reported by men whose business to serve the god of war.

To this awful score must be added the millions of strong men, the pick the race, who are butchered battle. In the early part of the last century Edward Irving figured that more people had been killed in war than were then living on the earth. Others have made the numbers larger. In modern times the genius of man has been taxed to the utmost to invent more effective means of destruction, and these are cited as evidences of advancing civilization. It would be difficult to cite a recent day of entire peace throughout the world. Larger armies than ever before have been forced into the field. Men have been hating each other and plotting death by every available means. Necessarily the work of killing has gone forward with increasing success. In the case of the recent big war the truth will never be known, but figures chiefly from official sources put the battle sacrifices to the god of war at 10,091,834 grown men.

No other god ever demanded so much. Sacrifice of wealth. Sacrifice of principle. Sacrifice of sentiment. Sacrifice of natural affection. Sacrifice of human comfort. Sacrifice of the best beloved. But the war god calls, and the deluded people follow on, as the rats and the children followed the fabulous Piper of old.

VI

The War God Identified

A god who has had so large a place in history, demanding so much and having his demands so eagerly met, is worthy of closer study. Every divinity whose name occurs in the early myths of the race is marked by certain attributes, which set him apart and indicate his relations to other beings. The god of war is no exception. From the oldest notions preserved in legends and folklore down to the latest displays on battlefields in Europe or Asia he is always the same, sinister in spirit, averse to happiness, anxious for misery and ruin. With tireless energy he arouses animosity, excites revenge, instigates murder, drenches the earth in blood and ditches it with the graves of the slain. He loves strife , as the huntsman loves the chase. He plays upon the base passions of men, and incites them to kill one another. In war he never considers the question of right, but allows either side to win by ferocity or shrewdness, trickery or the mere weight of numbers; and no scene is too sacred for his foul endeavours.

Through all the bloody history of the human race he has shown no variation in character. In it all he is disclosed as a god of lust and rapine, cruelty and crime, deception and hypocrisy, hatred and every base emotion that can move an immortal spirit. These qualities are closely linked together in the records, and only in general can they be disclosed in their separate foulness.

There is an obscure passage in The Revelation which seems to point the way. Using an indefinite past tense it says: "There was war in heaven: Michael and his angels to war with the Dragon; and the Dragon made war and his angels, and they prevailed not, neither was their place found any more in heaven. And the great Dragon, the old serpent, he that is called the Devil and Satan, the deceiver of the whole inhabited earth: he was cast down to the earth, and his angels were cast down with him."

However doubtful in some of its bearings the passage indicates that there was a spirit of evil which manifested itself in war in the eternal heavens; that the instigator and loser of that fight was called the Serpent, the Dragon, the Devil and Satan, and that after his defeat and expulsion he made the earth the scene of his activities, inflicting pain and woe upon the denizens of land and sea. In other Scriptures he is mentioned as making war.

These passages suggest what the scientists call a working hypothesis. Some of the early myths retain the name old Serpent, as indicating the adroitness and skill with which he wriggles himself into the affairs of men. In Egypt Sutek was accounted the source of all evil, both physical and spiritual, and he was described in terms that betoken the Devil of the Bible. The same character attached to Ahriman of Persia, Molech of Canaan, Ares of Greece, and the war god as named in other languages.

1. The god of war is always a god of lust. According to the Greek myth he was born of a desecration of the sex instinct, his parents being brother and sister. In harmony with such an origin he was further represented as seeking the love of Aphrodite, the wife of Hephaestus, herself the goddess of beauty and sex impulse, worshipped by rich men of Corinth in the sacrifice of their most beautiful female slaves. Dishonouring her own husband Aphrodite gave herself to the war god. She bore him two children named Panic and Fear, and they usually attended their father, as he directed armies and ordered fields of blood.

The Roman myth gave him a similar origin. It made him the son of Jupiter and Juno. It further connected him with the sex instinct. It was he who debauched the vestal virgin Rhea Silvia, and from the illicit embrace there sprang the Alban fathers, the Latin race and the walls of lofty Rome. The legends of other lands offer no divergent view.

These old myths disclose the deepest instincts of the race. They show a connection between the war lust and the sex lust. It indicates the struggle of nature to take care of herself and repair her ravages, the passion to kill being supplemented by the passion to reproduce. There is a natural bond between war and woman, but it is a bond desecrated and despoiled by the god of war.

The lessons of legendary lore are supported by the earliest testimony of history. In Eden the Serpent spoke to the woman, the only one in the world and she a man's wife. He spoke beguiling words, and led her astray. The record is meagre and euphemistic; the facts are not all disclosed, but whatever the meaning of the story certainly the first child born on earth was a true son of the war god, and he duly dipped his hand in his brother's blood.

The early conquerors rose to power, and forthwith established harems. David himself became a man of blood, and he proceeded in the usual path, taking many wives and concubines. The irregularities of famous warriors, such as Belshazzar and Xerxes, Alexander and Cyrus, Cæsar and Antony, Charlemagne and Nelson, are familiar to the students of history; and they seemed rather to add to the glory of military renown. Through all the annals of war followers of Aphrodite have hung about the camps, and have held high carnival with men in uniform.

When knighthood was in flower the jilted lover turned to war as the surest method of softening his lady's heart and winning her favour. In armour hiding his physical deficiencies he rode grimly away, leaving the parting message:

"If by the Saracen hand I fall
    Mid the noble and the brave,
A tear from my lady love is all
    That I ask for a warrior's grave."

The recent war, said by both sides to be a righteous war, was not free from unrighteous lust. In a public address to men a lecturer sent out by the Fosdick Commission said the French government asked Paris to furnish thirty thousand women to entertain soldiers at the front, and did not ask in vain. It seemed to be a patriotic duty to respond to such a call. It showed the proper devotion to La Belle France.

Speaking from personal knowledge Donald Hankey said: "Wherever there are troops, especially in war time, there are bad women and weak women, and the result is inevitable: a certain number of both officers and men go astray." A current poem represented a young man as relating what he saw in part in these words:

"I have seen the Devil in petticoats
        Tempting the souls of men;
I have seen sinners great sinners do great deeds,
        And turn to their sins again."

One of the popular songs for the boys in France was composed by a Red Cross nurse. It contained the following suggestive lines:

"In gay and wondrous Paris
        I have wooed the gay grisette;
I have courted Spanish maidens
        With hair of midnight jet;
I have flirted with the Irish girls,
        Whose eyes are twinkling blue,
And the bonny Scottish lassies
        Have heard my love song too;

With ardour I have courted
    A girl of English birth;
But in my thought of marriage,
      There's only one on earth."

The war god makes women of all lands his allies and his victims. He accords the gay grisette a place beside the faithful wife. After the signing of the armistice in 1918 the press dispatches reported that "the French women smothered the American soldiers with kisses"; and it was further reported from various sources that for once the negroes shared equally with the whites.

The patriotic spirit also moved among the women at home. A single issue of the War Work Bulletin gave these incidents: "When huge cantonments were slapped down by sleepy little towns, and thousands of handsome khaki-clad boys swaggered down the streets looking for a good time, the established social order was turned topsy-turvy. The startled mothers needed aid in directing the patriotic energy of their excited young daughters." Exactly. And it is said that in some instances the mothers also took on the patriotic excitement.

The official Bulletin further stated that clubs were instituted for two purposes: "First, through Red Cross work service, gymnastics and articulate ideals they furnished the girls with something to think of beside the romance of khaki. Second, they supplemented the individual homes in furnishing desirable gathering places where girls and soldiers played together. The girls faithfully performed club service, and became hostesses at soldiers' parties. Even girls who were nervous lest they get converted could not withstand a swimming tank or a hike or a weenie roast."

The Bulletin recorded also that many of the brides were very young, and had not grown up to their wedding rings. It cited two cases illustrative of many more: "A certain light-hearted damsel, loving one soldier loved all soldiers to her husband's acute distress. A fifteen-year-old bride with grey-green eyes and earrings as big as saucers wished at the end of a week of married life that she had gone on to school instead. Infinite tact was needed in dealing with those young married women, so conscious of their new dignity." No doubt of it.

The findings of the Fosdick Commission on Camp Welfare were not made public. However, in a private note Mr. Fosdick said: "Speaking in general it is well known that venereal diseases have always been in the armies of nations the dominant cause of disability."

In an article on "Life in an Army Training Camp" Frank Tannenbaum spoke from personal observation. His utterances were submitted to some two hundred officers and soldiers before publication, and were approved. On the subject of lust he said: "The soldier is very much concerned about woman. Just as gambling is one of the serious occupations of the soldier, so is the search after woman one of the great games he plays. It is the game of the huntsman, and like a good hunter he displays persistence, energy, avidity and resourcefulness in the chase. Generally speaking this activity in the pursuit of woman is not in vain, for by and large practically every soldier who participates in this activity, and a very large majority do, finds his efforts rewarded; and in this process he reduces all social institutions from the church to the gambling house to an instrument for his end, and does so deliberately."

Soldier Tannenbaum, speaking of the soldier's attitude toward woman in general, said: "It is the attitude of the scientist. It is an attitude shorn of modesty, morals, sentiment and subjectivity. It is immodest, unmoral, objective, evaluating and experimental. Men will sit till late at night in a darkened tent, or lie in their cots, their faces covered with the pale glow of a tent stove that burns red on cold nights, and talk about women but this talk is of the physical rather than the emotional, of the types, the reactions, the temperaments, the differences and the peculiarities of moral concepts, the degrees of perversity, the physical reactions, the methods of approach – as if it were a problem in physics rather than morals."

Dr. Curry had such things in mind when he spoke of camp conditions that "it would make common decency blush to describe"; but they belong to the war god's work. From the rape of the Sabines down to the day of the Fosdick letter armies have been full of filth. The instigators of war have always known it, but their purpose is better served by keeping the knowledge back from the unsophisticated public whose sons are wanted for the mill of death. The recruiting officer is not expected to tell. But the facts cannot be truthfully denied.

2. God of lust the war god is also a god of cruelty and crime. The atrocities reported from battle-fields in recent times are simply the old atrocities brought down to date and refined with the refinements of civilization. Elisha the prophet wept as he foresaw the cruelties that the heathen Hazael was destined to inflict on conquered and helpless Israel: "Their strongholds wilt thou set on fire, and their young men wilt thou slay with the sword, and wilt dash their children, and wilt rip up their women with child."

Such brutality was not confined to the heathen. Menahem, king of Israel in Samaria, marched against the city of Tiphsah: "Because they opened not to him, therefore he smote it and all that were therein, and all the women that were with child he ripped up." Under the sway of the war god it was obliged to be.

There has never been a war waged on earth that has not shown the same spirit of savagery. Religious wars, so called, have excelled in madness. and crime. Charlemagne ravaged Europe with fire and sword in campaigns of desolation that extended over thirty years or more. Fugitives were hunted down, captured, condemned and killed by thousands after they were disarmed. Eginhard, who was secretary to Charles and able to speak from personal knowledge, said Panonia was entirely depopulated, the situation of the royal palace utterly obliterated, the entire Hun nobility put to death, the glory of the nation destroyed and her treasures carried away.

Mombert mentions the cruelties enacted by Peter the Hermit in the first crusade. He says the robber, the incendiary, the criminal of every degree was offered the privilege of venting his base passions on the Saracens, and promised the martyr's crown if he died and the riches of those whom he slew if he survived. Allured by such prospects and driven by their lusts: "They ceased to be men. They sank below the level of brutes. Their insatiable bloodthirstiness exceeded that of tigers and hyenas. I deliberately weigh my words and scan their meaning. They understate the facts."

Motley records some of the cruelties committed by the Spaniards in the overthrow of the Dutch Republic, women and children and old men being butchered in countless numbers. The Spaniards seemed to cast off even the semblance of humanity and to assume the spirit of fiends. Infants were brained in their mothers' arms, parents were tortured in their children's presence, and brides beaten to death before their helpless husbands' eyes. Referring to the interruption of a wedding, the historian says: "The soldiers began by striking the bridegroom dead. The bride fell shrieking into her mother's arms, whence she was torn by the murderers, who immediately put the mother to death. An indiscriminate massacre followed. The bride was scourged with rods until her beautiful body was bathed in blood. At last alone naked and nearly mad she was sent into the city, where she wandered up and down through blazing streets among heaps of dying and dead, till she was put out of her misery by a gang of soldiers."

Cromwell made the streets of Drogheda run red with Irish blood. He turned victory into a massacre, and after the garrison had surrendered he caused thousands to be butchered with ruthless hand.

The recent stories of babes blinded from birth by heartless attendants, of little children maimed for life by cruel soldiers, of helpless women debauched and driven to loathsome tasks, of aged men mocked and murdered, of ministers of religion shot for mentioning mercy, of places of worship desecrated and rent into ruins, of waters polluted and made the means of agony and death, of millions of men the flower of the race ground into a bleeding and repulsive mass and dumped into trenches like the refuse of the shambles – all these terrible tales contain nothing new in the spirit shown; they simply show that the god of war has gripped the minds of the best educated people on the globe, and driven them to do his barbarous work.

It was a war of machine guns that mowed men down like grass before the scythe, of shells that killed scores in a single explosion, of mines that shot up horror from beneath, of aircraft that dropped destruction from above, of submarines that sank ship-loads of helpless creatures without warning, of depth bombs that caught the unsuspecting and snuffed them out, of mammoth guns that sent missiles of death into far-off towns, but it was all of the same spirit that moved the savage with his tomahawk and his scalping knife and his poisoned arrows. It was savagery brought down to date, and refined with the refinements of civilization. There was not a touch of human-heartedness in any of its work. Before the battle of the Marne Joffre commanded the men whose lives were in his hand to advance as far as they could, and when they could no longer advance to stand and die. It was a typical order. In spirit it was repeated in every army on the bloody fields. It was the acme of ruin.

There was also a report that Baron von der Keilhofer seriously suggested eating the flesh of prisoners. With the true spirit of a godless evolutionist he said the survival of the fittest and the idea of taking care of self were the ruling laws of existence; and in the presence of starvation he thought it would be the German duty to their brave soldiers and their families to slaughter such prisoners as Gott had given them, "as we would any other swine," to relieve their noble race, which according to his plan was confessed a race of cannibals. He cited the fact that the thing had been done before, but he expressed the hope that his people would be spared the necessity of eating their prisoners. Possibly the Baron was misrepresented, but nothing in the war god's character forbids such brutishness. His history records such deeds.

Will Irwin reported from abroad that the war, as it existed with its wholesale murder, was making brutes of men; that the laugh had gone out of the world, leaving people sad, sullen, and doggedly resigned to a bitter and relentless fate; and he also declared that the barbarities were shared by all the nations engaged. The war god is no respecter of persons. He debauches and brutalizes all who accept his service.

Mary King Waddington reported the ears of six German prisoners cut off; she said the Zouave who had done the deed, a mere boy, calmly asked the ladies if they did not want to see the ears, some of which he carried in his pocket. On being reproved for his gruesome cruelty the boy replied that he would always hurt and kill a Boche when he could.

Before a court convened to hear the evidence Gustav Voight testified that his squad approached five Belgian soldiers who expressed a desire to surrender, and found that they had two German soldiers bound with ropes. The Germans were hussars. One of the two drew attention to a third hussar hanging dead on a tree, his nose and his ears being cut off. The two hussars also said that the five Belgians were making ready to kill or mutilate them, if relief had not come.

Others testified of Belgian girls ten or twelve years of age armed with sharp instruments with which to inflict pain on wounded enemies. Sometimes the lobes and upper parts of the ears of wounded and helpless men were cut off in sheer cruelty. An orderly was shot to death by civilians firing from a schoolhouse, while he was engaged in bringing relief to wounded men in the yard.

The London *Times* spoke of the Kaiser as the bargaining beast; it said that there was no limit to German savagery, and advised that "we must fight the Hun with his weapons." It was simply savagery against savagery, and it was equally savage in either case.

With less excuse the same barbarous spirit prevailed here. In Chattanooga a Christian Association lecturer spoke to the men on the fighting spirit. As reported in the daily press he said it should be the object of every soldier to go over the top and get his man: "It's you and the other man. One of you has to go, and be damned certain that it is not you. The way for a soldier to bring his bayonet back is red, red with the blood of a Boche. It is a beautiful sensation to stick a fat German with a bayonet. When you fellows start to killing, you will take to it like a man takes to drink."

Proceeding the lecturer related the story of an English soldier who had captured a man: "In taking the prisoner to the rear the captor stumbled; seeing his opportunity the prisoner tried to make his escape, but the captor was too quick for him. The Boche threw up his hands and cried, 'Komerad, spare me, I have a wife and five children'; but the captor replied, as he thrust him through, 'You are a damned liar; you have a widow and five orphans.'" The report said the recital was greeted with rapturous applause.

Some preachers fell into the snare and became as brutal as the rest. In his own pulpit one of them said: "Every pro-German in this country ought to be shot. If you do not believe that I have the grace to do it, just give me a gun. If there is a man in this audience who does not believe in this war, I want to tell him he is a low down stinking skunk, and is not fit to sleep with hound dogs." It was true service to the god of war.

3. He is also a god of lies and all the forms of hypocrisy and deceit known the depraved heart. Here again the Germans have shown their efficiency. William Fisher of England writes a book on "The Villain of the World Tragedy," giving ample proof of German mendacity in the service of the war god. In one of his better books Henry VanDyke takes up the theme, and devotes some thirty pages to it. These gifted authors do not overdraw the picture. After all they have said probably less than half the truth has been told.

It is interesting to note that lying and deception of all kinds are expected in the service of the war god. The Peace Commissioners who traverse continents to meet in the million-dollar Carnegie temple at The Hague go through the solemn form of trying to make war as respectable as possible. For the purpose they prescribe certain rules, which always hold when there is no special reason for violating them. Then they practically annul their rules by saying: "The ruses of war are allowable."

These ruses which are determined by the combatants themselves include spies and their lies and their violations of ordinary military rules about uniforms and other matters, and their betrayal of confidences and all the diabolism and hypocrisy that depraved genius can invent. Honourable Peace Commissioners are not ignorant of these things. Ministers of religion know them. Knowing them they yet speak of honourable and righteous wars. They confess practically that there are honourable and righteous lies, honourable and righteous hypocrisy, honourable and righteous betrayal of confidence. They all admit that the enemy spy is a criminal worthy of immediate death, but they regard the friendly spy as an important factor in honourable and righteous war. It is the old fable of the gored ox set in terms acceptable to the war god. What is honourable and right for either side is a crime for the other side.

Sir Garnet Wolseley, at one time chief officer of the British armies, said: "As a nation we are bred up to feel it a disgrace even to succeed by falsehood; the word spy conveys something as repulsive as the word slave. We will keep hammering along with the conviction that honesty is the best policy and that truth always wins in the long run. These pretty little sentences do well for a child's copy book, but the man who acts upon them in war had better sheathe his sword forever."

The same high official further spoke of the difficulty experienced in managing spies; he said it was important that they should be unknown to one another, and suggested that each one employed be made to feel that he was the only one. He observed that some served for money, sometimes receiving pay from both sides, and that it was fortunate if one in ten imparted truthful information. The spy even among thieves is scorned, but in the service of the war god he is considered indispensable.

The public press recently gave the name and the picture of a man who had operated in Mexico both as a Mexican colonel and as a German captain; he pretended to be operating for the Germans with the Mexicans against the United States, at the same time he was making regular reports to the officials of our government. The government stooped to accept his services, and knowing the character of the man and his work the public press praised him and called him a patriot.

Mary Rinehart wrote a story called "The Amazing Interlude." It was the story of an American girl, who repudiated a devoted sweetheart, took all the risks of war time travel, pressed through picket lines and endured various hardships to get to Belgium and marry a foreign spy. The story was fiction, but it was true to life. The gifted authoress probably wrote out of her own heart. The liar and hypocrite who serves the war god is at a premium. Men who call themselves Christians put up money to pay such characters for their services.

It was not an accident that the story went the rounds of the great dailies, that the enemy were gathering up the mangled bodies of their dead soldiers, bundling them in wire like baled hay, carting them off to rendering establishments, extracting the grease from the forms of their dead to lubricate machinery, crushing their bones into fertilizer, feeding the flesh to pigs with the natural inference that later the pigs were used for food. The story was all a lie. Its character was known to those who gave it currency; but it served the base purposes of the god of war in stirring deep resentment in the minds of the multitude who are moved by their passions and blindly follow on in the paths which designing men wish them to take.

William G. Shepherd related this incident of a fellow correspondent who said: "Yesterday afternoon I attended the funeral of a hand. It was the hand of an old man, and it had been cut off by a German soldier. I'll bet I make the front page of the New York papers with my story this morning." Mr. Shepherd did not know whether the reporter made the front page or not, but he did know that the said reporter was playing billiards in a café when the grotesque funeral was said to have taken place. It was more important to make a sensation than it was to tell the truth. So the servant of the war god thought.

Under date of August 17, 1919 , W. T. Ellis said it gave a home-coming American a queer feeling to discover that a department of his own government could as shamelessly conceal or misrepresent facts as any of the European nations, whose intrigues and propaganda in the Near East disheartened Americans and menaced the peace of the world. Soldier Tannenbaum also said the talk about military discipline improving the morals of American soldiers emanated from sources that would place a wish above a fact: "The fact is that the soldier is very much more unmoral than when he entered the army, a fact that has very few exceptions."

4. Back of all these base qualities the war god is also god of hatred and the profanity and violence which hatred engenders.

"There are many kinds of hatred,
       As many kinds of fire;
And some are fierce and fatal,
       With murderous desire;

And some are mean and craven,
       Revengeful, cruel, slow;
They hurt the men that hold them
       More than they hurt the foe."

The war god indulges them all, and inspires them all. There has never been a physical war waged in love. The pretense of such a thing only illustrates the truth presented in previous paragraphs, that the war god inspires lies.

From the remote days when Hamilcar led his tender son to the altar and had him swear eternal hatred against the Romans down to last display of bitterness at home or abroad, the god of war has always stirred the passion of hate in the souls of men. The oldest records of the race attest the fact. Homer's Iliad, older than the psalms of David, glorifies deeds of violence born of hatred. The Old Testament itself seems to accord a man the right to hate his enemies.

Germans made a sort of fetish of efficiency, and Ernst Lissauer illustrated it in the finest Hymn of Hate ever set in human speech. It sounded the depth of depravity and measured the abyss of murderous desire. It was directed especially against England, but it equally expressed the antipathy felt toward all enemies.

It sprang into sudden popularity, and rose almost to the dignity of a national anthem. It was sung and lived, until the people were saturated with its bitterness. Under its evil power they fought and fell, and rose to fight again, a nation of seventy millions holding at bay six times their numbers including the foremost peoples on the globe.

Hate begat hate in the hearts of others. The Associated Press reported a German violently killed in a Paris garage. Ladies and gentlemen turned in from the streets, dipped their hands in the blood of the dead man, and ran out wiping it on the garments of passers-by and furiously screaming that it was German blood. Later the mother of a war baby killed her child; she was justified by the trial court on the plea that the child's father was a German soldier. Also a mother walking in a park with her child met a crippled soldier; turning to the child as if to impress her words, she said: "Do you see that legless man? The Boches did it, remember that!"

In the *Illustrated London News* Mr. Chesterton admitted the hatred, and said he shared it with other Englishmen: "Every man of us hated; if hate is wrong, every soul of us is wrong." In similar strain Dr. Orchard, a clergyman, said: "Does any one suppose that in the frightful struggles of a bayonet charge all soldiers do not have to put off the civilized gentleman and fight like devils? The truth is, behind every European man, not to mention the European woman, there is a savage; and if we are going to prepare for wars and wage wars, then we shall want the savage kept alive. With characteristic frankness and brutality this has been recognized in Germany. It has become a philosophy. In other countries, notably in our own, we do not discuss this sort of thing, but we depend on it."

The *Literary Digest* copied an article from Eben Phillpotts deploring the spirit of hatred that has swept over England, invading even the pulpit and contradicting the fundamentals of the Christian faith. He said the English proclaimed Germany's Christianity a spurious article and her people atheists and savages, while they were indulging identically the same spirit of blind antagonism.

Admitting the hatred, the London *Daily Mail* protested against its abatement. It said every man that preached the doctrine of forgiveness was helping the enemy to win a victory and making himself an accomplice in their wicked work. It declared such a man faithless toward God and perfidious toward men, and proceeded to brand him with the image of the Devil. Another great daily mentioned the swearing among the soldiers in Flanders, and said there was a noticeable spread of the habit in other circles, especially among clergymen, who were consigning the Kaiser to hell and dealing out deep damnation in good round oaths.

Among us there was less excuse for such hatred, but it swept over the land in great power. In the opening of hostilities an ardent militarist said we must learn to hate as the Germans hated, and must hate harder and make our hatred comprehensive enough to extend to everything German, the smell of German cooking, the sound of German music, the forms of German speech, all German products and the whole German race. He urged that we should send soldiers over the seas to do what Germans had done, giving them shell for shell, gas for gas, bayonet for bayonet, and paying them double in every respect: "We will hate until we are filled with hellish rage and fury of devils," said he.

The editor of a trade journal, widely copied and approved, used these bitter words: "Some men and women do not comprehend the meaning of this war. Some are pro-German, some are German spies, some are cowards who disgrace the mothers that bore them, some are just plain every-day fools, who should go out and root and live with swine in the field until the appointed time to be killed for the good of mankind. Is there anything on earth so craven, so bereft of soul, that it would be willing to parley with these accursed murderers and worse led by William the accursed?" Later, however, the same man admitted that there was great need for missionary work here at home. His bitter words implied as much.

Ministers of religion caught the infection, and some expressed a willingness to stab the Kaiser with their own hands. One left his pulpit to lecture workmen on their duties, and he instructed them to take anybody that tried to hinder their work out into the marsh, tie him down, place a bomb on his breast and send him to hell. Another arose in his pulpit and asked his congregation to join in saying: "To hell with the Germans!"

The willing audience rose to their feet and followed their spiritual leader in the profane imprecation which he proposed.

The service of such a god undermines the character of those who follow him. Not that all become utterly debased, but that all suffer debasement; and their debasement detracts nothing from their military glory, rather it seems to be expected. England withholds not a penny from the great monument reared to Nelson in Trafalgar Square because of his lustful attentions to Sir Hamilton's wife, and the knight himself accepted the unusual distinction conferred on him by the immoral Nelson. The sharpshooter is praised for slipping up on his fellow-man and killing him unawares. The spy is a hero according to the success of his efforts in lying and deception. Brutality in battle is rewarded with a *Croix de Guerre*. Jesus was murdered on a cross. Beholding as in a mirror the iniquities of war men are changed into the same image from baseness unto baseness.

There is genuine pathos in Donald Hankey's words: "A change comes over a man when his bayonet is red with the blood of his first victim. He sees red. The primitive blood lust, kept under all his life by the principles of peaceful society, surges through his being, transforms him, maddens him with a desire to kill, kill, kill." Hankey, whom love declared the most beautiful thing that ever happened, appealed to his companions in gore for confirmation of what he said. Later he fell a victim to the primitive blood lust of which he spoke.

William G. Shepherd told of things in Europe worse

than killing and being killed. It was men of families, of business, of ideals, of religion, all brought down to the same level. Like barrels whose hoops had been removed, these men had fallen apart in their lives and characters, and were like animals, like herded unthinking beasts; and at night in dreams he saw them, not as dead and mangled bodies, but as armies marching, each man wearing the head of some beast rather than his own. They were not leonine animals, but dumb, obedient, patient brutes, such as oxen, sheep, mules, dogs. He said it was worse than death; and sometimes as the men realized it all they stuck their heads above the trenches or used their own guns to end the sickening existence.

Far from such scenes Soldier Tannenbaum said the atmosphere of the camp deteriorated the sense of individuality, self-respect, interest and the thing that gives a man his fibre and grip on the world. He illustrated his meaning by the remark of a Sergeant Major who expressed gladness at being discharged and allowed to get out, explaining: "Well, it darn nigh makes a criminal of you, if you stay in it long enough." It does not pay to serve the Devil.

VII

God and the War God

God is the conscious and eternal Author and Finisher of all things. In the beginning he created the heavens and the earth and all that in them is. He is the God of gods and the Lord of lords, great and terrible, who neither regards persons nor takes reward. He is above all and through all and in all, and beside him there is none else.

In the Bible he is called by different names, according to the stages of human development and the urgency of human needs. In the original language of the Old Testament he is *ab* or *abba*, the Father for all his children. He is *bara*, the Creator of all things. He is *el*, the God of might. He is *elah* or *eloah*, like the Persian *allah*, the God who evokes the worship of rational creatures. He is *elohim*, the majestic triune God in whom all things consist. To Israel alone he is *yah* or *yahweh* (translated *Jehovah*), the conquering God of hosts, the first being a poetic form of the name. He is *adonai*, the Master who owns and guides the people of his pasture. He is *tsur*, the God who is as changeless as the rock.

In the Greek New Testament these names are repeated according to the varying needs of devout hearts, the definite article being generally used with each. He is *ktistes* or *ktisas*, the Creator; *pater*, the Father; *pantokrater*, the Almighty; *theos*, the God of all attributes; *kurios*, the Master; *soter*, the Saviour; *christos*, the Christ as God manifest in the flesh, whom to see is to see the Father.

In both Testaments he is revealed to the world as the God of peace. His instruction to Adam and Eve to be fruitful and multiply and replenish the earth is in direct contradiction to the war god's work, which destroys and decimates and depletes the earth. God who brought again from the dead the Lord Jesus, the great Shepherd of the sheep, through the blood of the everlasting covenant, is "the God of peace." The presence of the God of peace is invoked for the church at Rome and for all in their fellowship. The God of love and of peace is pledged to the church at Corinth and also to the church at Philippi. It is the God of peace who is implored by the apostle to sanctify wholly the church at Thessalonica. Also it is the God of peace who is destined to bruise Satan under the saints' feet, and make them perfect to do his will, working in them that which is well pleasing in his sight. He is one, and he changes not with the changing dispensations and the changing years.

The servants of the war god make a general appeal to the Bible, especially the Old Testament, in justification of what they call their glorious work . To the superficial they seem to say something, but to the thoughtful their sophistries clearly appear. The mere fact that the Bible says much about wars and rumours of wars in no wise indicates God's approval; nor does the record of wars waged by good men, such as Abraham or Moses, Joshua or Caleb, justify the conclusion that God approves of wars waged by men whom he has not authorized to make war.

The Bible has much to say about the gods of the heathen and the worship offered them. It records that Jacob the beloved allowed the images of strange gods in his house. It speaks of the worship of Baal and Ashtaroth and other heathen gods. It relates that the chosen people went after the gods of the people among whom they dwelt. It mentions Rimon, and the devotions offered him. It says Gideon, the captain of the famous three hundred, took the spoils of victory and built an altar to a Sidonian god. But no honest interpreter passes from these facts to the conclusion that God approves polytheism and idolatry. He allows them to exist, but he does not approve.

The Bible has much to say about polygamy and concubinage. Its faithful records show that men eminent in the annals of piety were lax in domestic life. Lamech, grandson of Enoch and grandfather of Noah, took unto him two wives, the name of the one being Ada and of the other Zilla. Abraham had as a concubine a servant woman, who was much at her master's mercy; and the godly Sarah approved the relationship until her own son was born. By that departure from domestic morality the father of the faithful became also the father of all the Ishmaelites in the world. Jacob took two wives of the same household, and all parties connected with the transaction seemed pleased. Moses was a polygamist, and the law given through him recognized polygamy as a fact and gave rules for its regulation. Among other things it provided that a man should not follow Jacob's example, and have two sisters as wives at the same time. Because of the hardness of human hearts and the consequent unhappiness in domestic life the law allowed a man to give his wife a writing of divorcement and send her away out of his house, but from the beginning it was not so. All these facts furnish no proof that God approves of polygamy and concubinage. The corrupt folks who incline to the Phallic worship known in the baser forms of heathenism do not justify their course by appealing to the polygamous practices noted in the Bible; rather they turn to Joseph Smith and his pretended revelation found in the Book of Mormon.

The Bible recognizes the existence of slavery. It shows that some of the chief figures in Bible history sanctioned slavery in buying and owning slaves and in having slave children born in their houses. Before the Levitical law there was a special command: "He that is born in thy house and he that is bought with thy money shall be circumcised." The law assumed the continuance of slavery, and set forth the relative duties of masters and servants. The divine plan included the slavery of Joseph in Potiphar's house, and of Jacob's entire race under Pharaoh. In various letters the Apostle Paul recognized the existence of slavery; he made no formal protest, nor did he counsel insurrection and bloodshed, rather he taught servants to obey their masters as they obeyed the Lord himself. God tolerated slavery, and saw men made in his own image marked with the lash of the taskmaster or bought and sold in the markets like beasts of the field, but he did not approve. His anger burned, and in due time he judged the nations that had committed the crime.

With a single exception the governments mentioned in the Bible were imperialistic. In the remote past Amraphel was king of Shinar, and Arioch king of Allasar. Before Abraham went out from Ur of the Chaldees the dynasty of the Pharaohs was established in Egypt, kings reigned over the Hittites and Abimelech sat on the throne of Philistia. Royalty was in evidence everywhere. From Moses to Samuel Israel enjoyed the only democracy known to the ancient world; they became dissatisfied with its administration and demanded a king, being willing to waste their heritage for the sake of being like the heathen around them. Christianity was born under the most imperialistic government the world had ever known, and it offered no sort of protest. But these facts all together do not prove that imperialism is God's ideal for human government, or that it pleases him.

Every page of the Bible recognizes the existence of sin in varied forms. The mere existence of a thing is no proof of divine approval. The Bible speaks of wars waged by the heathen, and wars waged by the chosen people both against the heathen and among themselves, and of wars and rumours of wars through the unfolding centuries; but these facts do not justify the general conclusion that wars instigated by men are in harmony with the divine will. There must be faithful study of the divine word to understand the mind of God on the matter.

There is no question about God's sovereignty. He has prepared his throne in the heavens, and his kingdom includes the universe. He is the supreme potter, and with boundless authority he makes of the same clay one vessel unto honour and another unto dishonour. He forms both the light and the darkness, and creates both the good and the evil. "Can there be evil in a city, and the Lord hath not done it?" He is able to bring a flood to sweep away ungodly millions, whose hearts are evil and only evil continually. He rains fire and brimstone from heaven, and destroys the incorrigible. It is sometimes his pleasure to "bring the sword upon a land," but always as a punishment for the land's iniquities. Jerusalem stoned the prophets and killed the messengers sent unto her; she knew neither the day of her opportunity nor the things which belonged to her peace, and God allowed her enemies to compass her about, and keep her in on every side, and level her even with the ground and her children within her, but he judged the nation that did the deed.

He held the hand of Cyrus the Persian, whom he called his anointed, and he said: "I will go before thee and make crooked places straight. I will break in pieces the gates of brass and cut in sunder the bars of iron, and I will give thee the treasures of darkness and the hidden riches of secret places, that thou mayest know that I, the Lord who called thee by name, am the God of Israel. For Jacob my servant's sake and for Israel mine elect I have called thee by name; I have surnamed thee, though thou hast not known me."

He pronounced woe upon Asshur, the name of the Assyrian war god and of the people that served him, saying: "Woe unto Asshur, the rod of mine anger, though the staff in his hand is mine indignation! I will send him against a hypocritical nation, and against the people of my wrath will I give him a charge to take the spoil and to seize the prey and to tread them down like the mire of the streets."

His first commandment expressed his eternal attitude toward the war god and all his works: "Thou shalt have no other gods before me"; but when men turned aside to serve the war god, he did not vacate his throne. He made the wrath and folly of man render him praise, and the excess of wrath he restrained. Cyrus and the servant of Asshur did not intend to please God in what they did: "He thinketh not so, neither doth he comprehend; rather it is in his heart to destroy and to cut off nations not a few. For he saith, 'Are not my princes altogether kings? Is not Calno as Carchemish? Is not Samaria as Damascus? As my hand hath found the kingdoms given to idols, whose graven images did excel those of Jerusalem and Samaria, shall I not do unto Jerusalem and her gods as I have done unto Samaria and hers?'"

The Assyrian king serving the war god was used as the rod of God's anger; but the war he waged was wicked in itself, and it did not escape the punishment which it deserved. When God's will was accomplished against Mount Zion and Jerusalem, God said: "I will punish the fruit of the stout heart of the king of Assyria, and dim the glory of his high looks. For he saith, 'By the strength of my hand and by my wisdom have I done it. For I am wise, and I have removed the bounds of people, and have robbed their treasures; and I have put down the inhabitants like a man of valour, and my hand hath found as the nest the riches of peoples, and as one gathereth eggs that are left so have I gathered all the earth, and there was none that moved the wing or opened the mouth or peeped.'"

On his part there was no recognition of God, and no desire to serve him. It was a case of the ax boasting against the hand that swung it, or of the saw magnifying itself above the arm that drew it back and forth. "Therefore shall the Lord of hosts send among his fat ones leanness, and under his glory shall he kindle a burning like the burning of fire; and the light of Israel shall be for a fire, and the Holy One for a flame. It shall burn and devour his thorns and briars in one day, and shall utterly consume the glory of his forests and fields."

God used the nations to punish Jerusalem and Samaria. He said: "The Babylonians and all the Chaldeans, Pekod and Shoa and Koa, and the Assyrians with them; desirable young men, captains and rulers, great lords and renowned, all of them riding upon horses, and they shall come against thee with chariots, wagons and wheels, and an assembly of peoples that shall set against thee, buckler and shield and helmet round about; and I will set judgment before them, and they shall judge thee according to their judgments. And I will set my jealousy against thee, and they shall deal furiously with thee. They shall take away thy nose and thy ears, and thy remnant shall fall by the sword; they shall take thy sons and thy daughters, and thy residue shall be devoured by fire. They shall also strip thee of thy clothes, and take away thy fair jewels."

In the service of the war god they fulfilled what was written of them; but they were not guiltless in the things which they did, and in due time God punished them for their crimes. He alone holds the supreme authority "to kill and to make alive," and he has never surrendered any part of it to any class of his creatures. In the past he sometimes appointed certain persons to kill or to raise the dead, but he allowed such deeds only by the authority which he directly bestowed. Out of the bloody and rebellious nations of heathenism God chose a people for a possession. Unto Abraham he said: "Get thee out from thy country and from thy kindred and from thy father's house into a land that I will show thee, and I will make thee a great nation, and will bless thee and make thy name great." He repeated the promise to Isaac and Jacob, saying to the last: "Israel shall be thy name." He claimed the children of Israel for his own. When they grew and multiplied in numbers sufficient to make up national existence, he led them forth, and gave them laws that were to govern their national life. He said: "Hear, O Israel, the statutes and the judgments which I speak in your ears this day, that ye may learn them, and keep and do them." He spoke primarily to the nation as a whole, and then to the individuals composing the nation, and he gave the specific word: "Thou shalt not kill."

The prohibition was set in unlimited terms. It forbade his people taking the initiative in destroying human life anywhere. It withheld from them the right on their own responsibility to take what they could not restore. Only as he himself gave specific authority were they allowed to kill their fellow-men created in the image of God.

Savage militarists and devotees of the war god have sometimes set up the claim that the Hebrew term *ratsach*, used in giving the commandment, is a narrow term, which forbids what is defined as murder and does not forbid other kinds of killing; but in the court of candid investigation the claim cannot be sustained. The term is not the most common in Hebrew usage, but it has not the limits which the bloodthirsty have endeavoured to put upon it. The record speaks for itself.

Solomon uses the word to indicate the act of a hungry lion in killing a man: "A lion without! I shall be *ratsach*-ed in the streets." Certainly a lion may kill a man, but a lion does not commit murder. For rational creatures capable of recognizing divine authority, the law forbids what the lion does to a man.

The psalmist chooses the word to express the deed of thoughtless persons who wreck a man, as mischievous youths might cast down a leaning wall or a broken fence: "Will ye *ratsach* him down, all of you, as a wall inclined, as a fence that is thrust down?" Beasts sometimes pounce upon the sick or wounded of the herd; the thoughtless sometimes trip the tottering to a fall, as a leaning wall is overthrown for the excitement of seeing it tumble, and such acts are included in the prohibition of the commandment, but they do not come under the technical definition of murder.

The term *ratsach* is used also to indicate the wicked deed of the Gibeonites in their treatment of the Levite's concubine. It was a base proceeding, and the woman died from the things which she suffered; but there was no malice in the hearts of the sinners, and no purpose on their part to take the woman's life. The lust that impelled them was not blood lust, but it brought death and worse than death to its hapless victim. Surely it was forbidden by the law, but it was not murder in the usual sense of the term.

There is yet further disproof of the sophistry that the *ratsach* expresses only the killing that is murder. Referring to the use of cities of refuge the law says: "That the slayer might flee thither, who should *ratsach* his neighbour unawares, and hated him not in times past." It further says: "The revenger of blood shall *ratsach* the slayer," and it proceeds to state definitely that such a deed is not murder, being authorized by the Ruler of the race: "He shall not be guilty of blood," though his act is recorded in the term *ratsach*.

Not always is the converse of a proposition true; but

149

if *ratsach* is the exclusive term for the crime forbidden in the sixth commandment, there was not a murder committed in the first two thousand years of human history. On this assumption Cain did not murder Abel: "Cain rose up against his brother Abel, and *harag*-ed him." He left his brother a corpse, his blood crying from the ground; but according to the war god's champions his deed did not fall within the prohibition of the sixth commandment. There were only two men of military age in the world; Cain marched against his brother and conquered, leaving the enemy dead on the field, but on the baseless assumption that the Hebrew term *ratsach* indicates the only forbidden killing, Cain did nothing contrary to the law of God.

Esau hated Jacob for the treatment he had received from him, but under the limitations set upon the sixth commandment by the lovers of blood he did not contemplate murder when he said: "The days of mourning for my father are at hand, then will I *harag* my brother Jacob." Neither did the sons of Jacob transgress the law, when they violated their covenant with the Hivites, and came upon the city and slew all the males, butchering innocent and guilty alike. Their deed was not recorded in the term used in the sixth commandment. Nor did they propose to murder their brother Joseph, for their base purpose to kill him because of their envy and fear was not expressed by the term *ratsach*. Reuben delivered Joseph out of their hands, saying: "Let us not kill him," and he used yet a different word. The deed proposed was the same by whatever term indicated, and every candid and competent mind knows that all such deeds are forbidden by the law which says: "Thou shalt not kill." Disobeying by wholesale is only compounding the iniquity.

God has made man in his own image, and he holds the right of life and death in his own power. He deprecates the assumption of that right by any man or any set of men. He says human bodies in right relations are his temples, and he forbids their butchery and destruction: "If any man destroy the temple of God, him will God destroy, for the temple of God is holy." It is a fearful sentence against the champions and servants of the war god, their chief business being to mar and ruin the bodies of men. Their military education, their knowledge of tactics, their skill in engineering, their power of endurance, everything distinctive in their lives goes for nothing, unless in the end it makes them more effective for the work of destruction. And God has revealed his righteous and changeless hatred of them and of their destructive deeds. He will finally destroy.

"The mills of God grind slowly,
     But they grind exceeding small;
And though with patience stands he waiting,
     With exactness grinds he all."

With true insight Byron represented the Devil as exulting in the sickening scenes of the battlefield. Out on a drive one day, as the bard conceived it, the Dragon came to the place where men were butchering one another in remorseless cruelty:

"Then long and loudly laughed he:
'Methinks they have here little need of me,
    They are doing my work so well'
    For the field ran so red
    With the blood of the dead,
That it blushed like the waves of hell."

It was a harmonious conception, the Devil rejoicing in pain and desolation and ruin. It suggests the saying attributed to Wellington: "Except a battle lost, there is nothing more melancholy than a battle won."

God has made of one blood all nations of men, and it is impossible for him to see brother men butchering one another without what the Bible calls repentance and grief in his heart. A chaplain in the recent orgy of blood gets at the heart of the matter in the following lines, which he puts into the mouth of a plain soldier boy, who looks upon the cold form of his young friend lying among the mangled dead:

"And the lovin' God looks down on it all:
    On the blood and the mud and the smell.
O God, if it's true, how I pity you,
    For you must be livin' in hell.
You must be livin' in hell all day,
    And livin' in hell all night.

I'd rather be dead wi' a hole in my head,
    I would, by a long, long sight,
Than be livin' wi' you in a heavenly home,
    Lookin' down on yon bloody heap,
That was once a boy full of life and joy,
    And hearin' his mother weep.

The sorrow God feels must be hard to bear,
    If he really has love in his heart;
And the hardest part in the world to play
    Must surely be God's part.
If he knows the things about this trench,
    The mud and the blood and the pain and the
        stench,
It must surely break his heart."

Mr. H. G. Wells adopts the Zoroastrian view that God is struggling with forces that are beyond his control, doing the best he can, but failing to keep the world in order. The truth is set forth in the word: "All day long have I stretched forth my hand to a gainsaying and disobedient people." He calls men to right ways, but they refuse; he extends the beckoning hand, but they disregard; he gives them counsel, but they heed it not. He allows them to walk in the ways of their own hearts and in the sight of their own eyes, but he gives assurance that for all things he will bring them into judgment.

God, who gives to all life and breath and all things, has the right to withdraw his gifts. He reserves to himself alone the right to inflict death, and in the exercise of his right he uses any means pleasing to himself: beasts of the earth, famine, fire, flood, forces of nature, pestilence, serpents, wars whether waged by the heathen contrary to his will or by his own people appointed to execute his wrath against sinful nations. He invariably judged the nations that went to war without his authority, and he took the responsibility for wars waged by his own people according to his will.

He said unto Moses: "I am Yahweh; I appeared unto Abraham, unto Isaac and unto Jacob as God the Almighty, but by my name Yahweh was I not known unto them. Also I have established my covenant with them, to give them the land of Canaan, the land of their pilgrimage, wherein they were strangers. I have heard the groanings of the children of Israel, whom the Egyptians have kept in bondage, and I have remembered my covenant. Therefore say unto them that I am Yahweh; and I will bring you from under your Egyptian burdens, and I will rid you of their bondage. I will redeem you with an outstretched arm and with great judgments. I will take you to me for a people, and I will be your God. Ye shall know that I am Yahweh, your God that bringeth you from under the burdens of the Egyptians."

For the conflicts destined to ensue it was a distinct disclosure of Yahweh as Israel's war god: "Yahweh is a man of war; Yahweh is his name." The clear promise was given: "Yahweh shall fight for you, and ye shall hold your peace." He was further revealed as the Lord of hosts, the leader of armies. His presence was symbolized in the ark of the covenant, and wherever it went in harmony with his will it was a token of victory. Under Yahweh's guidance and in his strength the conquest of Canaan was accomplished with a ruthlessness rarely surpassed in the annals of war. The crimes of the heathen were great. Their sacred rites partook of gross immorality. Their continuance was an offense to the Almighty, and he sent his people to destroy them.

In every such case, however, God made his will clear. He left nothing to be inferred. He called Abraham in unmistakable terms. He spoke with equal clearness to Isaac and Jacob. He talked with Moses face to face. He instructed Joshua and Caleb, Barak and Deborah, Samson and others in terms that left no room for doubt. He has never commissioned any other nation or people to make war. Charles J. Gitteau presumes or he plays the hypocrite, when he claims that God has sent him to kill a man; equally do the modern war lords presume or play the hypocrite when they claim that God has sent them to kill thousands. In either case the claim is a baseless assertion.

The matter is easily put to the test. In all the campaigns and battles of the Old Testament there is no case in which God led his people to defeat, and no case in which he lost a man in a battle conducted according to his will.

The earliest battle in which God led his people is mentioned in the fourteenth chapter of Genesis. Chedorlaomer and other kings were at war with

Sodom and Gomorrah. They took all the goods of their enemies, the booty including the person and property of Lot. The matter was reported to Abraham, and immediately he gathered his servants and pursued the victors. With his household servants he made an attack on the allied armies of the kings, and drove them back to Hobeh. He recovered the goods and the captives, and brought them back in triumph. Abraham was the friend of God, and God gave him an easy victory.

The next definite conflict put record came in connection with the deliverance from Egypt. Pharaoh's armies pursued after the departing slaves. God commanded his people do nothing, but to stand still and see the salvation of the Lord. They obeyed and saw, and in the raptures of easy, conquest without loss to them they sang: "Thy right hand, O Yahweh, hath dashed the enemy in pieces. In the greatness of thine excellency thou hast overthrown them that rose up against thee. Thou sentest forth thy wrath and consumed them as stubble."

Entering upon the wilderness journey they encountered many enemies. One of the first to give battle was Arad, king of the Canaanites. "Yahweh hearkened unto the voice of Israel, and delivered up the Canaanites, and utterly destroyed them." The place of the battle was known as Hormah, which means destruction.

On the borders of the Amorite territory Moses sent messengers to ask the privilege of passing peaceably through the land. Sihon, the king, refused. Battle ensued. "Israel smote him with the edge of the sword, and possessed his land from Arnon to Jabbok." All the cities of the Amorites in Heshbon and in the adjacent territory were taken, and the victors proceeded by the way of Bashan. Og, king of Bashan, gathered his armies and went out to meet them. God said: "Fear not, for I have delivered them into thy hand, him and all his people and all his land, and thou shalt do to him as thou didst to Sihon, king of the Amorites." The incidents became historic. Years afterward the psalmist gave glory to God, who slew great and mighty kings for Israel's sake, Sihon, king of the Amorites, and Og, king of Bashan, being mentioned by name.

In the closing days of his career Moses was sent to avenge Israel on the Midianites. He took a thousand men from each tribe according to the word of the Lord. The five kings of Midian were slain, also Balaam the false prophet. Spoils of cattle and other things were taken, and cities and castles were burnt. The spoils of men and beasts were brought and delivered unto Moses and Eleazer the priest.

After the leadership passed to Joshua God said: "There shall not a man be able to stand before thee all the days of thy life; as I was with Moses, so will I be with thee." Under the new leadership the first notable battle was fought at Jericho. There were no heavy ordnance, nor machine guns, nor deadly weapons of any kind. Rams' horns constituted the equipment, and they were filled only with vibrant air. The people obeyed, and God did the rest. The event became a monument to faith rather than physical courage, and in the later centuries an apostle said: "By faith the walls of Jericho fell down, after they were compassed about seven days."

The host went forward with never a backset, except when they failed to honour God. Adonizedek, king of Jerusalem, became alarmed at what was coming to pass. He entered into a league of protection with four other kings. The Lord said unto Joshua: "Fear them not, for I have delivered them into thy hand." And it was so. "The sun stood still and the moon stayed, until the people had avenged themselves upon their enemies; and there was not a day like that before it or after it, when Yahweh so hearkened to the voice of man, for Yahweh fought for Israel."

Other rulers took alarm. Jabin, king of Hazor, sent messengers to neighbouring kings asking for a league of defense against the invaders. But God reassured Joshua: "Be not afraid because of them, for to-morrow about this time I will deliver them up all slain before Israel." It came to pass according to the word. Also Joshua cut off the giants of the mountains, and overcame them. The entire list from Og down to Tirzah included thirty-three kings and their armies. The Lord gave unto Israel all the land of Canaan, "and he delivered all their enemies into their hand."

After the death of Joshua the leadership fell to Judah. "Judah went up, and the Lord delivered the Canaanites and the Perizzites into their hands, and they slew of them in Bezek ten thousand men." Judah proceeded further against Hebron, and slew both rulers and subjects, and made desolation of their cities and their goods. They took Gaza, Askalon and Ekron and all the adjacent territory. They drove out the inhabitants of the mountain, but they disobeyed God and failed to drive out the inhabitants of the valley.

Sin brought disaster, but God raised up men to deliver his people from their enemies. Among them were Othniel, Ehud, Shamgar and others. In a day of darkness Gideon was called, a man who in the beginning of his career was lacking both in religious faith and physical courage. Reassured by miracles and messages Gideon at last marched forth with an army selected by God himself. It consisted of just three hundred men against an army of one hundred and twenty thousand and more; the rabbins regarded the three hundred as the cowards of the crew, men who lacked the moral courage to retire at the given opportunity, and lacked the physical courage to stoop down and drink like men, but lapped up the water like trembling curs. Josephus said: "There were three hundred men who took water tumultuously," as if afraid to drink calmly in the presence of their foes.

Later the people of Israel repudiated the kingship of God, but he did not yet repudiate them. He continued to hearken to their cries of distress and to show himself gracious to their needs. He gave Saul some victories. Through Jonathan and one other young man he put thousands to flight. He attended the movements of David, and lavished blessings on the nation that had rejected him. In the days of Hezekiah he still showed his willingness to send deliverance asked in humility and faith. Sennacherib came up against Jerusalem with a vast army. The helpless Hezekiah called no army at all; he appealed to God, and received assurance: "He shall not come into the city, nor shoot an arrow there, nor come before it with shield, nor cast a bank against it. By the way that he came shall he return, and he shall not come into the city, for I will defend the city to save it." That night God sent his angel to smite the foe, a hundred and fourscore and five thousand men. Byron celebrated the event in the familiar lines:

"Like the leaves of the forest, when summer is green,
That host with their banners at sunset was seen;
Like the leaves of the forest, when autumn hath
　　blown,
That host on the morrow lay withered and strown.

For the angel of death spread his wings on the blast,
And breathed in the face of the foe as he passed,
And the eyes of the sleepers waxed deadly and chill,
And their hearts but once heaved, and forever
　　grew still.

* * *

The widows of Asshur are loud in their wail,
And the idols are broken in the temple of Baa,
And the might of the Gentile, unsmote by the sword
Hath melted like snow at the glance of the Lord."

The second point of the test to which men who pretend to be fighting God's battle must submit is equally impressive. After the slaughter of the kings Abraham returned from the fight bringing all his servants, not one missing. In his conflicts with Pharaoh Moses lost no one. Except in the cases of disobedience and sin no one was killed in the conquest of Canaan. Gideon used no deadly weapons, but he brought back his entire three hundred, leaving a hundred and twenty thousand dead on the field. Jonathan and his armour bearer routed the army of the Philistines, but they received no wound. They found that there was no restraint with the Lord to save by many or few.

The Old Testament to which militarists appeal discloses another impressive fact, that every battle lost was a sign of God's displeasure in what was being done. God cannot be conquered in battle. He is able to make the earth open her mouth and swallow up his enemies, or to marshal the elements against the wicked, or to incline the stars in their courses to fight his battles, or to withdraw his breath and let them die, slaying them without any weapon whatever.

In this matter the Scriptures use great plainness of speech. At Kadesh it was said: "Because ye are turned away from the Lord, therefore the Lord will not be with you." In the face of the warning they presumed to go out to battle, and the result was inevitable. They were beaten, for God was not with them. Later Moses reminded them of their sin in rejecting the warning:

"Go not up, for am not with you." Their defeat showed that they were displeasing to God.

The first battle of Ai showed the same thing. There was one grafter in the camp, and they were defeated with loss of life. God explained: "The children of Israel could not stand before their enemies, but turned their backs, because they were accursed." Their defeat and loss indicated God's disapproval. When the Philistines smote Israel and killed four thousand men at Aphek, the elders knew the disaster indicated God's displeasure, and they said: "Wherefore hath the Lord smitten us to-day before the Philistines?" It was on account of their sins; they were smitten again, and the dreadful news caused Eli to fall to his death.

Later Israel formally rejected God, choosing to be like the adjacent heathen. After that, except when God was especially invoked and his presence promised, the race was to the swift and the battle to the strong. God maintained his throne in the heavens, but he did not fight Israel's battles for her. The result was that Israel never attained unto the fulfillment of the promise in becoming the ruling nation of the earth. David at his best was not the equal of other great monarchs of ancient times. Solomon in all his glory was not the most glorious ruler of that age, and in the next generation the power of the war god rent his kingdom in twain. Disasters multiplied for each division of the chosen people who had broken their covenant with God, and desolations followed each other in swift succession. The Northern kingdom, comprising the larger numbers and retaining the name of Israel, set out to maintain itself after the manner of the heathen, and in about two centuries and a half its entire population passed from the pages of history. Taking the sword contrary to the will of God, they perished by the sword.

> "Like the dew on the mountain,
>   Like the foam on the river,
> Like a bubble from a fountain,
>   They perished, and forever."

The sin that wrecked them was the rejection of God, that they might be like the heathen around them, killing and being killed. From time to time God showed himself willing to be gracious and to resume the leadership from which he had been deposed: "O Israel, thou hast destroyed thyself, but in me is thy help." He besought them with promise: "Return unto me, and I will return unto you"; but he pleaded in vain, and his deluded people continued to plunge down the abyss.

David was exalted from the sheepfold to the throne; but ruling over a people who had rejected God he conformed to their ideas and warred after the manner of the heathen, and like them he sometimes won and sometimes lost. In the forty-sixth psalm distinct protest was made against such methods, but it was made in vain. There are different texts and different versions of the line which is usually rendered: "What desolations he hath made in the earth!" Farrar Fenton, an English scholar who read the Scriptures only in original tongues forty years, translates that and the previous line:

"Come gaze on the works of the Lord,
What power they show to the earth."

The Septuagint, a Greek version made a thousand years and more before the date of the oldest extant Hebrew text, uses *terata*, meaning wonderful things, in the place of the term rendered desolations. Others hold that the line is a vocative, calling those who work desolations to witness the different works of the Lord. All the texts and versions, however, come to the same practical end. God, who uses no weapons of any kind to win in war and forbids the killing of men by others, did a wonderful thing in the world, or caused consternation among the devotees of the war god, by stopping deeds of blood and destroying the instruments of the hateful craft: "He maketh wars to cease unto the ends of the earth; he breaketh the bow, cutteth the spear in sunder, and burneth the chariot in fire." It was a decisive blow to such as got glory and wealth by the shedding of blood, but such was said to be the work of the Lord, and men were called to behold.

David heard the call and beheld, but he continued his wars in the usual way. He had some measure of success, but it unfitted him for the holier task which he wished to accomplish. Having built a kingdom by war he was not build for the God of peace. He approached the coveted task, but his hopes were dashed the ground.

God said: "Thou hast shed blood abundantly and hast waged great wars; thou shalt not build house unto my name because thou hast shed much blood upon the earth in my sight."

After Judah alone remained a broken remnant of a disobedient people, the shedding of blood went on. Under the sway of the war god that remnant sank lower than the brutes, and Isaiah was constrained to say: "The ox knoweth his owner and the ass his master's crib; Israel doth not know, my people doth not consider." He saw them a sinful nation, a seed of evil-doers, a people laden with iniquity, their country desolate, their cities burned with fire, their religion a farce, their prayers unanswered. The only specific charge against them was: "Your hands are full of blood." It was the stain gotten in the service of the war god, and it became the symbol of all iniquity: "Your sins as scarlet, red like crimson." It was the deep hue of the blood they had spilt, as they went forth butchering and being butchered contrary to the will of God.

God's will was made clear, but it was disregarded, and the bloody work of war continued. Later Isaiah repeated his old charge: "Your hands are defiled with blood." Ezekiel also was called to judge the bloody city, and he said: "The city sheddeth blood in the midst of it, that her time may come." He saw the better classes under the power of the war god: "Her princes in her midst are like wolves ravening the prey to shed blood, to destroy souls, to get dishonest gain." The ministers of religion turned traitors to God's holy cause, and

Ezekiel said: "There is a conspiracy of her prophets in the midst thereof like a roaring lion ravening the prey; they have devoured souls, they have taken the treasure and precious things, they have made her many widows in the midst thereof." Naturally with such spiritual leadership the common people also took to blood, and men carried tales and took gifts to shed blood.

Their bloody deeds were attended by the inevitable incidents of war. There was contempt of holy things, profanation of the sabbath, oppression of the poor, vexation of the fatherless and the widow, and the unspeakable lewdness that the war god always incites. "One hath committed abomination with his neighbour's wife, another hath lewdly defiled his daughter-in-law, another hath humbled his sister, his own father's daughter." The patriotic profiteer also got in his usual work: "Thou hast taken usury and increase, and thou hast greedily gained of thy neighbours by extortion, and hast forgotten me, saith the Lord God."

The result was bound to come. And God said: "I will gather you, and blow upon you in the fire of my wrath, and ye shall be melted in the midst thereof. As silver is melted in the midst of the furnace, so shall ye be melted; and ye shall know that I the Lord have poured out my fury upon you."

The sentence was suspended for a season. The depleted race was preserved, that the promised Prince of Peace might appear. He came unto his own, and his own received him not. They rejected him, as they had formerly rejected the God of Peace from ruling over them. It marked the end, They were cut off, and driven like chaff before the wind according to the word: "I will scatter thee among the nations and disperse thee among the countries."

It has come to pass according to the word of the Almighty, and the word shall stand. Not all the millions of Baron Hirsch nor all the might of British armies shall be able to reverse the divine decree. To this day the veil is upon Israel's heart, when the Scriptures are read. Only when their heart shall turn to God shall the veil be taken away. Only then shall they be admitted to their heritage in the Promised Land. So it is written, and so it must be. Otherwise the word of God is made of none effect.

VIII

Jesus and the War God

Jesus on earth was God manifest in the flesh. He came as the only begotten Son of God. All things were made by him, and without him was nothing made that came into being. Originally of the substance of God and equal with God in the eternal heavens, he thought it not a prize to remain in the heavenly abode; he humbled himself and assumed the form of a servant, and was made in the likeness of man. He was in the world, and the world was made by him, and the world knew him not. He said: "I and my Father are one." He claimed all authority in heaven and in earth.

These things are clearly taught in the Scriptures, which Christians profess to believe. Every man who accepts them knows that in the use of physical force Jesus would have been invincible. According to the record he had legions of angels at his command. His authority extended to the powers of hell, and unclean spirits were subject to his word. He ruled nature's forces, and winds and seas obeyed his will. He had power to provide all dainties for an army, as he provided food for hungry thousands in desert places. He was master of disease and death, and without medical aid he was able to heal every sick or wounded man and even to raise to renewed life every man killed in battle or dead of disease. In him was life, and the life was the light of men.

With boundless resources at his command and with infinite power under his control he yet eschewed the methods of the war god. The idea that he at any time resorted to violence to enforce his will contradicts the word which reviewed his career from its close and declared: "He had done no violence." Such an idea is born of passion, the wish being father to the thought; it is a practical denial of the absent Lord, and is not in harmony with the facts. On the mountain Jesus encountered one called the god of this world, who claimed its kingdoms and their glories and also the right to dispose of them as he would; tempting Jesus he said: "If thou wilt fall down before me (in adoration and submission to my will and ways), all shall be thine." The offer was real, else it contained no temptation and the record of it as such was a deception and a fraud. Jesus met it as real, and rejected it with disdain. He lived under the most imperialistic government known to ancient times, but instead of plunging his people into bloody and devastating war to overthrow imperialism, as some pretended apostles of righteousness have done, he supported his imperial government and taught his disciples to do the same, at one time working a miracle to pay the required tribute. He based his course upon an eternal principle, which he fully understood and faithfully applied.

Truth cannot be established by physical forces. It is possible to kill those who hold distasteful views, whether of religion, science, government or any other matter; but it is not possible to convert them by violence. Mohammed may kill off the Christians of Asia and Africa with the sword, and in their room he may train up in the faith a new generation that never knew the truth; but he cannot make one real convert by butchery and blood. Peter the Hermit and his later imitators may adopt the great Arabian's methods and start on their bloody crusades, butchering Mohammedans by the thousand, but they convert nobody, and the thing which they introduce to the new generation is as worthless in spiritual life as the thing which they have displaced. The willing tools of ecclesiastical bosses may compel helpless men and women to submit to baptism in the name of the holy trinity, but the brutal process does not make one true Christian. Oliver Cromwell, whom historians call hypocrite, traitor, usurper, regicide, may redden the streets of Drogheda and other places with Catholic blood, but his brutalities enacted with the divine name on his lips neither destroys Catholicism nor establishes any other form of Christian faith; they only dishonour the name of the Lord, and make it a hissing among those without. With quaking nerves Galileo in sackcloth may kneel before his tormentors and loudly abjure his doctrine concerning the earth's movements; but his convictions remain the same, and in his liquid Italian he says to himself, *E pur si muove*: "It does move though." The recent fury has killed many junkers and thousands more of their supporters; but it has not directly changed anybody's thinking on the subject, nor has it brought any nation any discernible good. Violence expresses passion rather than thought. The minds of men cannot be coerced. This every candid and competent man knows beyond a doubt.

Jesus as a teacher sent from God naturally understands the case, and he is too strong and holy to be diverted from the truth by any popular outcry or current emergency. He retires from the clamour that would make him a king and leader of armies, and adheres to the methods of peace. The consensus of unbiased opinion, whether Christian or not, unfalteringly recognizes him as the Prince of Peace, whose entire influence is contrary to the war god and all his works.

In this matter the Scripture passages that indicate the attitude of Jesus may be set into three classes. They are prophetic utterances which tell beforehand what his character and influence were destined to be, historic records which preserve his personal teaching and conduct, and apostolic writings which interpret and enforce his doctrine. Some of these are here recalled:

"Behold, a virgin shall conceive and bear a son, and shall call his name Immanuel.

"The government shall be upon his shoulder. His name shall be called Wonderful, Counsellor, Mighty God, Everlasting Father, Prince of Peace. Of the increase of his government and of peace there shall be no end.

"In his days shall righteousness flourish, and abundance of peace so long as the moon endures.

"His name shall endure forever; it shall continue as long as the sun, and men shall be blessed in him.

"He shall redeem their souls from violence, and precious shall be their blood in his sight.

"The wilderness and the solitary place shall be glad for them, and the desert shall rejoice and blossom as the rose; it shall blossom abundantly, and rejoice even with joy and singing.

"And they shall beat their swords into plowshares and their spears into pruning-hooks; nation shall not lift up sword against nation, neither shall they learn war any more.

"But they shall sit every man under his vine and under his figtree, and none shall make them afraid.

"They shall not hurt nor destroy in all my holy mountain, for the earth shall be full of the knowledge of the Lord, as the waters cover the sea.

"Behold, I bring you glad tidings of great joy, which shall be to all people. For unto you this day is born in the city of David a Saviour, who is Christ the Lord.

"And suddenly there was with the angel a multitude of the heavenly host praising God and saying, Glory to God in the highest and on earth peace, good will toward men.

"And Jesus came to Nazareth where he had been brought up; and as his custom was he went into the synagogue on the sabbath day, and stood up for to read. And there was given unto him the book of the prophet Isaiah; and when he had opened the book he found the place where it is written: The Spirit of the Lord is upon me, because he hath anointed me to preach the gospel to the poor, he hath sent me to heal the broken-hearted and to preach deliverance to the captives and recovering of sight to the blind, to set at liberty them that are bruised and to proclaim the acceptable year of the Lord.

"And he began to say unto them: This day is this scripture fulfilled in your ears.

"Blessed are the peacemakers, for they shall be called the children of God.

"Ye have heard that it hath been said, An eye for an eye and a tooth for a tooth; but I say unto you, That ye resist not evil, but whosoever shall smite thee on thy right cheek, turn to him the other also.

"Ye have heard that it hath been said, Thou shalt love thy neighbour and hate thine enemies, but I say unto you: bless them that curse you, do good unto them that hate you, and pray for them that despitefully use and persecute you.

"Be ye therefore merciful, as your Father also is merciful.

"The Son of man is not come to destroy men's lives, but to save them.

"And he that hath no sword, let him sell his garment and buy one.

"And they said, Lord, behold, here are two swords; and he said unto them, It is enough.

"And one of them smote the servant of the high priest, and cut off his right ear. And Jesus said, Suffer ye thus far; and he touched his ear, and healed him.

"Then said Jesus unto Peter, Put up again thy sword into the sheath.

"Thinkest thou that I cannot now pray to my Father, and he shall presently give me more than twelve legions of angels?

"My kingdom is not of this world; if my kingdom were of this world, then would my servants fight that I should not be delivered unto the Jews.

"God hath made of one blood all nations of men to dwell on all the face of the earth.

"Whosoever hateth his brother is a murderer, and we know that no murderer hath eternal life abiding in him.

"He that loveth not his brother whom he hath seen, how can he love God whom he hath not seen?

"Ye do well if ye fulfill the royal law according to the Scripture, Thou shalt love thy neighbour as thyself.

"Love worketh no ill to one's neighbour, therefore love is the fulfilling of the law.

"Bless them that persecute you; bless, and curse not.

"Recompense no man evil for evil. Dearly beloved, avenge not yourselves.

"If thine enemy hunger, feed him; if he thirst, give him drink. Be not overcome with evil, but overcome evil with good."

To dispassionate judgment these inspired words can have but one meaning. They speak with clearness and power. They tell of a kingdom of peace and purity, kindness and love, in which the god of war and lust, cruelty and crime, lies and hatred, has no part; a kingdom in which two swords are enough, which has had but one armed soldier and him commanded to sheathe his blade when he had struck but a single blow. They forever mark Jesus who was crucified as a pacifist, who chose to die rather than resort to violence and the shedding of human blood. Heaven and earth shall pass away, but his words shall not pass away. They abide forever, and by them shall he judge men at the last day.

Christians who followed next after the apostles knew the teaching and spirit of Christ. In the second century Justin the devoted martyr said: "The devil is the author of all war." Others renowned alike for piety and learning approved the saying. Later Celsus the Epicurean fiercely assailed Christianity, charging among other things a lack of patriotism, because its adherents declined to take up arms and kill men over political ques tions. Origen, surnamed Adamantius, made reply, and justified the refusal of Christians to bear arms on the ground that the teaching and spirit of Jesus were against war.

For three hundred years the dominant spirit among Christian people was against war, the prevailing sentiment being expressed in the words of an eminent martyr, who refused to serve in the army, saying: "I am a Christian, and cannot fight, if I die." It is related that Marcellus, a Roman centurion, was converted; at once he resigned his place in the legion, saying he had become a Christian and could not continue in the work of war. He was imprisoned, and later put to death; but he remained true to the faith.

Clement of Alexandria called Christians the followers of peace, and said they used none of the implements of war. Lactantius also affirmed that it could never be lawful for a righteous man to go to war. After the faith had spread far over the empire, Tertullian said not a Christian could be found in the Roman armies. He was strong in the idea that Christ forbade war. He cited passages that have already been quoted, and said that by disarming Peter Christ disarmed every soldier.

In his day Irenæus said Isaiah's prophecy was fulfilled, and Christians had changed their swords and lances into instruments of peace and knew not how to fight. Another historian said Christians refused to attend the gladiatorial shows, lest they should become partakers of the murders committed there.

When Constantine departed from the faith, and resorted to violence in the name of Christ, he prepared the way for the crusades and the dragonnades and all the cruelty and persecution that have marred the pages of history and disgraced the name of Christ; but through all the centuries of violence and desolation there have been devout souls who have cried as voices in the wilderness in earnest protest against the crimes committed in the service of the god of war. Pages of such protests might be given, but they would avail nothing in the minds of those who reject the plain teachings of Jesus.

Some of the recent war literature has been remarkable in its effort to subvert the Scriptures and set Jesus among militarists and champions of the war god's work. In rare instances the design has been clearly stated; in others it has appeared in doubtful analogies, in rhetorical questions and in subtle appeals to the base passions of men. Though the stress of the conflict was milder here than abroad, the literature here seems more dogmatic and passionate than that of English writers.

The reasons for this may be found in part in the unexpected conditions that arose. In 1916 the people re-elected a president on the plea: "He kept us out of war." When the popular will as expressed at the polls was ignored and the country. plunged into war, those who assumed the right to take the tragic step distrusted the people's patriotism for volunteering the national defense. Under the guidance of a militarist they hurriedly enacted an arbitrary conscript law. By the might of statutory enactment they alienated the inalienable right of liberty and the pursuit of happiness for millions of helpless citizens. Under the guise of democracy they resorted to Prussian methods, but they did not remove the difficulties nor make the way clear.

The Christian sentiment of the country had to be reckoned with. There were in the country some twenty millions of persons, for the most part mature in years, who named the name of Christ, worshipped him as the Son of God, and confessed him the guide of their lives. It was not the functional Christianity which finds its expression in creeds and confessions, in art and architecture, in rites and ceremonials, in genuflections and postures, in the fashion of clothes and the cut of hair; it was a matter of personal experience and clear conviction. In the atmosphere of freedom men did not receive their religious opinions from ecclesiastics and functionaries; they read the Bible for themselves and learned directly the teaching and spirit of Christ, and their souls revolted at the things that were rudely forced upon them.

Under the coercion of the conscript act many young men whose lives were hallowed by songs of peace on earth obeyed the compulsory call in joyless mood. The espionage law smothered the constitutionally guaranteed liberty of speech, but it was powerless to check the inevitable flow of thought. Some who started out with a certain elation engendered by the noise of hired clackers were speedily disillusioned. Awakened by the brutalities of the military system always the same, which robs men of the right to regulate their own words and deeds and in the end drives them forth to kill their fellow-men who also are driven to kill, they felt every Christian principle and sentiment rising up in solemn protest. It was not that they were afraid to die. O, no; they simply shrank from befouling their souls with the blood of other young men who were as helpless as themselves to resist the brutal system under which they groaned. The novelty of a trip abroad with a pompous escort of bristling war ships, with the blare of brass bands and the roseate writings of hired sophists, did not quiet the cry of conscience, and some who sailed away with a pale imitation of enthusiasm speedily rose to the conception that the whole thing was irreparably wrong and utterly subversive of the principles taught by Christ.

The situation was serious. It furnished a rare opportunity for the multiplication of Iscariots, who were willing to betray the Lord for a price. Ungodly Germany had led in other iniquities, and again she became the exemplar for certain ministers of religion who made their pulpits recruiting agencies for the army or turned away from the church to urge the bloody service of the war god. Men who for years had contended for the separation of church and state openly repudiated or silently ignored what they had professed, and hurried away to get state commissions to preach under state direction and for state pay. Naturally they were expected to make their preaching conform to the plans of the government rather than the teachings of the New Testament. They preached the righteousness and glory of war, and some went so far as to promise on their own responsibility a crown of immortality to such as died in their efforts to kill their fellow-men.

Less brazen in their treason to Christ others undertook to effect a compromise between the Gospel and the work of the war god. One author freely admitted that it was necessary to go beyond what Christ had said for evidence that he in any way approved the war god's cruel work; and that he proceeded to do. In the state of mind to which he came he found no logical difficulty in passing from a whip of small cords for sacrificial animals in the temple court to poisoned gas and big betsies and machine guns for the battle-fields of Europe. One militant boldly accused Jesus of failing to practice what he preached, saying: "Jesus did not turn the other cheek."

Mr. Roosevelt, who was in no sense a theologian, discredited the divinity of Christ by assuming that he was a mere child of the times, who did not speak for the ages and the nations, but simply addressed himself to local conditions. He said the Gospels did not deal with war at all; that there was no war in Judea during the time they covered, and no question arising from the need of going to war. It was an easy way out, but it did not lead to the light. He further said: "The only way successfully to oppose the might which is the servant of wrong is by means of the might which is the servant of right." It was a restatement of what the German war lord, Bernhardi, had previously said: "Behind the law stands the state armed with power which it employs, and rightly so, not merely to protect, but actively to promote the moral and spiritual interests of society." Bernhardi, however, recognized a fact which Mr. Roosevelt ignored, that above the rivalries of states there is no impartial power to decide on questions of right and wrong. In war every belligerent judges its cause to be just, and Mr. Roosevelt's remarks apply with equal force to either side.

Dr. R. E. Speer, a sort of attaché of the government, tried to justify the Christian in taking up the brutal work of war; but a good conscience forced him to confess: "Yes, war is contrary to the teaching and spirit of Jesus." He was sure the nation that instituted a war was violating the law and the mind of Christ. At that point he dropped his place as a teacher and trailed off into a question which he did not try to answer: "When it has been done, and war violating Christ's principles and disregarding and dishonouring his love has been let loose, then does it follow that his teaching and spirit require that free and unhindered course shall be given it?"

Mr. Wells, who avowed himself an ardent pacifist, ran into the same blind alley. He found that his views were like the seed on stony ground; they had no root in themselves, but depended on what somebody else would do. His Mr. Britling had no convictions of his own, but regulated his conduct by what others did. He was for peace conditionally. Was he for honesty conditionally? Was he for sobriety conditionally? Was he for chastity conditionally? Was he for truthfulness conditionally? Or, to follow the current fad of bringing in the sex question, was he for virtue on the part of his wife and daughters conditionally? To all such questions Dr. Speer and Mr. Wells would answer with an emphatic No. Why then be for peace conditionally? When somebody else repudiates the teachings of Christ and plunges into wicked war, why follow the unholy example and compound the iniquity?

The match in the incendiary's hand never starts a conflagration of itself. Only when it collides with some resisting body does it flare up into a consuming flame that brings destruction and ashes, poverty and woe. One army may overrun a country, but one army never makes a war. Dr. Speer and every other thoughtful person knows this, and hence the question which appeals to ignorance and to the spirit of revenge which lies so deep in the human heart. It is always the second army that causes the crash. The spirit is the same, whether in the first or the second, and it is the second that Jesus especially forbids: "Resist not evil. Unto him that smiteth thee on the one cheek offer the other also." There are always enemies who strike; it is the second blow that makes the fight. Avenge not yourselves is the word. Give God a chance.

Dr. Speer further honoured his intelligence and his conscience by confessing the disparity between his teaching and the word of Jesus. He predicted a day when war would be "an anachronism, a long abandoned evil of barbaric times." In anticipation of the better day to come he said: "This book that I am writing, if a copy should remain until that future day of peace, will seem a sad and pitiful thing to any one of its happy citizens who may chance upon it." Even now it seems as sad and pitiful as Peter's denial of his Lord, and has much less to justify it. Peter was ignorant and panicky; he was outclassed in the presence of his enemies, and he had not the written word of his Lord to sustain his trembling faith.

Dr. Forsyth of England was required by the spirit of loyalty to support his country in the war that she waged. He was constrained to confess it contrary to the teachings of Jesus, but he justified the course on the ground that people generally have not accepted the Gospel of Christ. He said "It is more didactic than useful to tell us that war is the renunciation of Christian ethic. Of course it is. But that would be a good consideration to offer only if mankind were Christian. It would then be to tell them that they were renouncing their own moral principles."

Dr. Forsyth and thousands more, however, do claim to be Christians. They are placed in the world to be true to their Lord in the midst of a crooked and perverse generation. By his example and teaching Jesus has made it possible for them to be loyal to the government under which they live and at the same time loyal to him. He instructs them to render unto Cæsar the things that are Cæsar's, to meet the obligations which the government lays upon them, the government itself assuming responsibility for its acts so long as it lasts. Equally does he instruct them to render unto God and not to Casar the things that are God's. Every Christian is bought with the price, and he belongs to God through Jesus Christ. When Christian men voluntarily give themselves up to the foul work of war and willingly partake of its cruelties and crimes by offering their means to make it effective, by Dr. Forsyth's own confession it is quite to the point "to tell them that they are renouncing their own moral principles" and betraying their Lord.

The idea that the individual Christian may wait on the conduct of others to determine his own course is subversive of the entire Christian system. Jesus stressed individual responsibility. He repudiated the notion that a man might regulate his obedience by what another did: "What is that to thee? Follow thou me." He knew the spirit of the unconverted, and compared them to wild beasts that raven the prey. Knowing all things he did not instruct them to provide themselves with poisoned gas and big betsies and machine guns and high explosives to kill off the beasts and make the world safe for sheep. Contrary to current thinking he said: "Behold, I send you forth as sheep in the midst of wolves; be ye therefore wise as serpents, and harmless as doves."

The disposition of men who profess the name of Christ to slump and slack under the pressure of passionate clamour recalls the pathetic words of the English Archdeacon, J. Patterson-Smyth, uttered in the very heat of the conflict: "Remember first what this war is emphasizing: that it is not Christianity that is to blame, but the lack of it. We are finding out that the world has been contenting itself with a thin veneer of Christianity, and that only a small minority anywhere are living deeply the Christian life." Nowhere has the lack of the deep spiritual life been more glaring than in the conduct of men that have turned away from the gospel of peace and love to preach the doctrine of war and hate. Their course has inflicted a wound that only God can heal.

This veneer Christianity, as the Archdeacon calls it, this pseudo faith seething with passion and bathed in blood, has engendered the indifference of the agnostic and evoked the scorn of the infidel through the ages. The lancing logic of Voltaire, the stinging sneer of Diderot, the biting sarcasm of David Hume and the torrid rhetoric of Robert Ingersol indicate the contempt which it has excited among sinners whom Jesus came to save.

The last fury that swept over the world has been scornfully called a Christian war, since it involved especially the nations that have rather boasted of their Christian civilization. Replying to a proposal from the Episcopal Church that the Jews become Episcopalians, a learned rabbi cited the fact that Christian people had pillaged and injured and slain his people in the most fiendish manner, officers of the church pronouncing their maledictions and underlings lighting the fagots and burning Israel alive in the name of the God of love. He specifically asked with scorn; "Why shall the Jew accept Christianity? What are its superior claims? Has it abolished war? Has it fostered human brotherhood?" He even questioned the sincerity of those who asked him into the Christian fold, saying: "What proof have we that you yourselves have accepted Jesus? Did he teach persecution? Did he teach national savagery and international barbarism? You may believe in him in theory, but in practice you have defied him."

And there is ample ground for the rabbi's taunt. Knowing the teachings of Jesus and yet believing in war the German Nietzsche showed at least the Christian virtue of intellectual honesty; as a scholar he was not willing to play the hypocrite, and he frankly repudiated Jesus as an inspired teacher and guide. It is a base and ignoble thing for men to seize the respectability that inheres in the Christian name and then repudiate the principles that made the name honourable. The men who knew Jesus and the men who knew his personal acquaintances were willing to face the cruelest martyrdoms the world has ever known rather than take the sword in self-defense; those who were ready to call down fire from heaven upon their enemies received the Lord's rebuke in meekness, and learned to suffer scorn and pain and death rather than betray him and his word, and it is base treason to their memory and to the Lord whose spirit they bore for any man to intimate by word or deed that twentieth century civilization knows a better way.

The most egotistical militarists seem to concede that God made the world, furnished the raw material, so to speak. They regard the divine accomplishment, however, as incomplete and unsatisfactory. To their lofty conceit, which sometimes approaches the borders of madness, it does not seem a safe world for their favourite forms of government respectively. On the one hand it is not quite safe for imperialism, and on the other not quite safe for democracy. They agree that it is a crude sort of world, which ought to be made over according to their higher notions of how a good world ought to be run. They further agree that Jesus, who is sometimes credited with the making of the world, proposed a plan for obliterating oppression and injustice and filling the whole earth with the knowledge and glory of God as the waters cover the sea, and that his plan did not include violence and hatred and butchery among men. They have a plan which they consider superior, but it is not in harmony with the teachings of Jesus; and necessarily something must be done.

The imperialists are bold enough to put sentiment aside and reject the authority of Jesus entirely. They calmly consign the records that indicate his divinity to the realm of fable and fiction. They speak kindly of him as a young man of uncertain origin, who had no early opportunities for education and no social standing, who also said some very good things, but collided with the authorities and was soon put out of the way. With a patronizing smile they pass up the idea that he speaks with any sort of authority for them or for any one else. Their premises being granted, they have an easy and effective method of settling the matter. Apart from its destruction of Christian faith their method commands the respect of all who admire fearless thinking and consistent conduct.

Militarists who assume the Christian name have a more perplexing situation to meet. Against their course they have not only the teachings of the Scriptures, but also the protest of eminent Christian men through the centuries from Justin the martyr down to David Starr Jordan the author and educator. Thomas J. Morgan, himself a soldier, is constrained to say that Jesus as the Prince of Peace came to bring peace on earth and to establish good will among men, that the entire spirit of the New Testament is the spirit of peace and that every true preacher of righteousness is a preacher of peace. George Truett, one of the best beloved men on the two hemispheres, declares in a public address that war is ghostly and atrocious and ought to come to an end. These militarists who hold to Jesus admit all these things, but they are not quite ready to quit. If the world were only what it ought to be, and if the Turks and Huns and other heathen would get converted and set the example, they also would take Jesus at his word and put up their swords without wounding another man; but as things are, the Lord must wait. In the idiom of the moral slacker mentioned in the ninth chapter of Luke's narrative they. are willing to say: "Lord, I will follow thee; but let me first go and stifle my wicked enemies with poisoned gas and smash them with exploding shells and wreck them with machine guns and send them to hell, so the world may be safe for democracy." And Jesus told the other slacker that the man who put his hand to the plow and looked back was not fit for the kingdom of God. Then wounded in the house of would-be friends he steadfastly kept his face toward Jerusalem, and quietly passed on to bear his cross and be killed.

The inconsistency of these militarists who claim Christ is clear to every thoughtful mind. It arises from lack of faith in the effectiveness of what Jesus taught. It is a practical denial of his divinity and of his ability to meet the emergencies that arise among men. It is a concrete confession that the Christian system is not suited to a sinful world, and can be made effective only after leading sinners like Turks and Huns have been killed off. The rabbi notes it. Fearlessly facing the future, speaking for the race that gave Jesus to the world and for thousands more who stand without, he openly charges that these bloody Christians have defied the authority of the teacher whom they have urged upon him as the Son of God and the promised Messiah. Before the withering charge they stand speechless, or they answer in disingenuous and evasive terms; possibly they take up a collection to hire somebody to convert the Jews.

Nevertheless Jesus abates not a jot nor a tittle of what he has said. He has spoken with the authority of God, and not as the scribes; but in mercy he stoops to explain and to justify his inhibition of war. He does not create a new truth, nor does he issue a divine decree to work mischief in the earth; he simply discloses the thing that is forever true. He says the sword, the symbol of armed force of every kind, is an instrument of destruction and ruin, which wrecks those who use it as well as those against whom it is used: "They that take the sword shall perish by the sword."

The truth that he reveals to the trusting provincials who gathered about him and hung upon his words reveals itself to the broader culture that is familiar with the lessons of history and taught in the ways the nations have taken. So far as the record has been preserved, whether in formal chronicles or faded inscriptions, preserved on bricks and monuments or kept in crypts and tombs, the nations that have flourished and faded, Hittites, Philistines, Amorites, Hyksos, Medes, Persians, Babylonians, Assyrians, Arabians,

Tyrians, Sidonians, Carthegenians, Israelites, Spartans, Saracens, and all the rest, each and every one perished under the violence represented by the sword. The famous empires of Pharaoh and Darius, Alexander and Cæsar, Charlemagne and Frederick, Louis XVI and Napoleon, took the sword and perished by the sword. Nothing was ever built on violence that in due time did not provoke a greater violence to sweep it away. There never breathed braver men than those who followed the Stars and Bars from Fort Sumter to Appomattox, or men surer of the righteousness for which they fought. They deliberately abandoned the only field in which they could make an appeal to the principles of righteousness, and turned to the field wherein might is the measure of right. It was the oft-told tale. And taking the sword the Southern Confederacy perished by the sword.

Competent observers say the world is in a worse condition to-day than ever known before. Nations that were great and prosperous and happy a few brief years ago are desolate and stagnant and starving. Farms are devastated, fields barren, factories idle, houses dilapidated, men discouraged, women hopeless, children famishing for food. The spirit of turmoil and unrest is abroad, and men's hearts fail for fear and for apprehension concerning the things that are yet to come upon the earth. The false and foolish promise to end violence by committing violence has not been fulfilled; blood flows in many lands, and the world staggers beneath its intolerable load.

The whole unspeakable condition has been produced because the nations foremost in the line of advancing civilization were too dull to learn the lessons of history and too wicked to hear the voice of God. Repudiating alike the word of the Lord they became alike guilty in his sight. In their madness they seemed to vie with each other in their haste to tumble into the pit of war, and one by one they received the punishment that was appointed for their sin. Rejecting the truth and taking the sword, they perished by the sword.

If France, for example, ruthlessly smitten as she was by a nation that had openly rejected the teachings of Jesus, had had the judgment to heed the lessons of history or the religion to obey the law of Christ, and instead of meeting iniquity with iniquity had offered no resistance whatever, it would not have been a thing new under the sun. Various cities of Asia Minor opened their gates to the debauched and brutal Alexander who trampled peoples beneath his bloody feet, and allowed him to go his godless way. Jerusalem, city of the great king, sent her high priests in gorgeous robes to meet the drunken and lustful wretch and escort him into the town, and so allowed him to pass by with as little harm as possible. Others who had not the wisdom of Jesus to guide them somehow found the right way, while some foolishly took the sword and perished by the sword. Babylon herself opened her famous gates and admitted him to her palatial precincts; and in a few years her wisdom was rewarded in his death by his own excesses.

For a while Russia fought the invading Napoleon,

and invariably fell before his brutal legions; but at Moscow her passion somehow subsided, by luck or inspiration wisdom prevailed, she declined to fight, and won the victory that destroyed Napoleon's power. Out of his magnificent army of six hundred thousand men some thirty thousand famished and frosted wretches staggered home, and the imperial Corsican's fame was smitten with a deadly wound.

Had France learned the lesson and refused to take the sword, it seems certain that she would have been overrun, but not with marauding millions aroused to vengeful fury. Certain also that she would have been thrown back to her ancient form of imperial government, and would have paid her state taxes for a time in Berlin rather than Paris, the two cities being hardly a day's journey apart. Was that too great a sacrifice to make, if in return she could have alive the million and a quarter brave men who were killed in the strife, their wives and children homed and happy, the land at peace, business prospering, and no burden of war debts to crush the people for generations to come? Let candour and wisdom answer. As for the wounding of national pride, there is never a wound but rather a sense of dignity in the consciousness of acting on principle and even suffering inconvenience and harm for the sake of the things that are right.

Pathetic indeed is the lot of Premier Clemenceau. While the passion was on, and he was leading his people into the ruin that has come, his admiring friends called him the Tiger, a treacherous and feline beast of prey. He seemed to appreciate the compliment, and increased his fury in the work of butchery and blood, getting even with Bismarck, who was dead and did not care. A cruel cat sometimes devours its own family. When the victory was won, and his own people duly wrecked in the way which he publicly confessed, the end had to come. The tide of passion began to ebb. Human feeling struggled to life in the French breast. Beasts of prey seemed dangerous among widows and orphans; the Tiger was left in his lair, and a man was called to guide the people in the ways of peace. Like others originally, created in the image of God the Tiger, dripping in the blood which he caused to be shed, must stand at last before the judgment seat of Christ.

France is mentioned especially, but in no invidious spirit; simply as illustrating the case of all. Every nation that took the sword suffered loss far beyond any discernible harm that could have come from following the teachings of Christ. Our own nation was unexpectedly plunged into the strife in the way already described, but there is in the public mind no clear understanding as to why it came about. Our two most distinguished citizens, Wilson and Taft, give different versions of the matter, and the people are equally confused. But there is no uncertainty about the results. More of our citizens were killed by war accidents and by the mysterious "other causes" mentioned in official reports from France than were drowned from all the British ships sunk by Germans. A hundred thousand more died in battle and by disease, commerce was disrupted, labour disorganized, money depreciated, law dishonoured, property seized, taxes increased, and burdens of debt laid upon a loyal people which generations unborn and innocent must repudiate or struggle to pay, blood money every cent.

More than this. Christianity has been discounted in the minds of thousands, as they have seen men scorned and ostracized and sometimes cast into prison for holding to the doctrines of Christ and opposing the cruelties of war. Millions of money gathered to the tune of John Brown or any other tune do not atone for the past. The world cannot be converted by hired proxies. What communion has light with darkness? What concord has Christ with Belial? If righteousness can be established by violence, the gospel of kindness and love is preached in vain. If citizens are true to Christ in killing off sinners through their governments, they are equally righteous in killing off sinners through their mobs, especially if they are orderly mobs that march with soldierly tread. The logic is inexorable, and in a single State of the Union in 1919 twenty-one sinners were lynched. Certainly if there had been no sinners there would have been no lynchers of sinners. But in it all Jesus is mocked and crowned with thorns. And his changeless word is fulfilled, that they who bite and devour one another are bitten and devoured.

IX

The War God Repudiated?

The subject is introduced with a question mark. In the consideration of the current talk about

> Carrying his name away,
> And dropping it into the bottomless pit,
> To await the judgment day,

it is worth while to keep in mind the character of the war god and his amazing skill in warping the thoughts of men. Sometimes the talk is born of poetic fervour, and is backed by nothing stronger. Sometimes it issues from the hearts of pious men, who lack the moral strength to live by their convictions and in times of passion fall away. Sometimes it is made to please sentimentalists who shudder at pain, and is fitly defined by the slang term bunk. Sometimes it is merely what the French call camouflage, and is designed to conceal a sinister purpose.

Many of the people who talk fluently about ending war appeal to nothing fundamental, and give no reason whatever for what they propose. They seem to think that the course of history may be reversed and the war god balked in his brutal designs by a vigorous use of the dictionary. The League Covenant, which has had so much discussion in the Senate and elsewhere, proposes to achieve international peace by the acceptance of obligations not to resort to war; but in the entire document, which seems to have cost this country alone about four hundred dollars a word, there is not the slightest hint at a reason why nations should not resort to war or why peace should be preserved. It lays down no principle whatever for its guidance, and much of its pompous phraseology is as inane as the solemn utterance of an ignorant Christian Science reader who said mortal mind which was nothing was conscious of being some-thing, and salvation consisted in revealing to mortal mind that it was nothing! The instrument gives no evidence at all of a serious purpose to end war.

Through the centuries war has elevated men to positions of emolument and honour, that were quite beyond their reach by any means of personal worth. It has set men of coarse fibre and common mould in company with the truly great, and has adorned with coveted laurels men of corrupt mind and depraved heart. And there is a question if the world is willing to abolish so easy a road to fame.

There are influential classes of men who are ardently opposed to such a proposal. The junkers are not confined to Germany. They infest every prosperous land, and cast their baleful shadows over its fairest scenes. Everywhere they are loyal servants of the war god, and they resent any effort to limit his power or dim his glory. By his service they have not only their wealth, but also their honours, pleasures, travels on land and sea, banquetings with women and wine, easy exemption from obligations to morality, superiority confessed by obsequious underlings and eternal salvation promised by unfaithful ministers of religion. Like the silversmiths of ancient Ephesus, they are quick to oppose any marring of their prospects, and from their point of vantage they are easily able to fire the ignorant mind and set the multitude in an uproar of vociferous praise to their favourite god.

The German junker makes no secret of his views. He openly and boldly proclaims the glories of war, and sneers at such as oppose him, calling them old women in breeches. In England the same spirit in milder degree is disclosed. Edward Dicey and Lloyd-George say in so many words that annexation of territory and consequent war are quite proper, if they promise material advantage to the empire. The question of right and wrong is ignored, and the matter of gain made supreme. The spirit is illustrated in all the oppressive history of England. As late as 1914, according to a public charge made by Joseph W. Folk, Great Britain seized the Egyptian government, and later proposed to reduce Egypt to the condition of a subject nation, exercising the sort of protectorate that a highwayman claims over his victim's pocket-book. Through its official organ the American Navy League sounds the same note. It says imperial ambition is essential to national effectiveness. It glorifies war. It sees in pacifism and national kindness marks of degeneracy. Practically it adopts the teachings of Prof. von Laschau, of Berlin, that the struggle for supremacy is better than the concord induced by brotherhood, and national jealousies and conflicts sources of freedom and progress.

In all lands army and navy work together for the flag and a larger appropriation. These millions who loaf at public expense most of their lives are ready to move at the slightest sign of danger to their craft. Near them are blood kin, family connections, beneficiaries, flunkies, constituting in all a considerable following, who are usually in sympathy with the men who wear gaudy uniforms and wave nodding plumes. There seems to be in the military spirit something tending to the fantastic. Dr. Curry mentions the fact that in 1849 there was not in the entire neighbourhood of Baden a chicken cock that had not been robbed of its tail to adorn the headgear of the vain and swaggering sons of Mars. And such flashy dress catches the crowd and makes friends for the god of cruelty and crime.

There is another powerful class whose interests are closely linked with the soldier's trade. They are the money grubbers, who rush for government contracts and sinecures, and pile up bloody millions, while they shout for national honour and free institutions. A great ammunition company sends out a big cartoon showing one of its mammoth plants in full operation, and under the firm name is written the legend, Empire Builders; but there is no hint of the destruction and misery that attend their work. Easily recalled are the stories of embalmed beef, dog bread, sleazy clothes, leaky overcoats, inferior shoes and other cheap supplies sold to the government at exorbitant rates for the use of soldiers who had no recourse against the treatment they received. In all these men the love of money is stronger than the love of their fellow-men; and they are ready for the thousands to be ground in the war god's cruel mill, if thereby they can pile up larger wealth. If they think of stopping war at all, it usually is thought that it cannot be done; and in proof they point with power to the past.

The money grubber's influence in connection with war has some illustration in our own brief history. In 1807 President Jefferson recommended an embargo on war supplies intended for angry nations of Europe, that were butchering each other with savage fury. Agnostic though he was called, he felt that it was unethical to share their iniquity by furnishing them for a price the means of destroying one another. The embargo was duly placed. The money grubbers took offense. All that Jefferson had done to free the colonies and establish the government weighed but little against the offense of hindering trade merely to save human lives. He was vociferously denounced, the tide of public affection was stayed, and the author of the Declaration of Independence retired at the end of his term in deep disfavour. It was a warning to all successors in the presidency.

In recent years there was a brief embargo on arms for turbulent Mexico. It pinched the gur makers. They appealed to what is called international law, which seems to exist for the benefit of trade instead of the people. The embargo was lifted. The gun makers got the money. The Mexicans got the guns. Later they used them to kill our citizens; and the imperial order to take the bandit Villa dead or alive was laughed to scorn.

President Wilson was bitterly opposed for a second term because of his pacifist views. For the same cause he received enthusiastic support. He appeared before a great audience in advocacy of his claims, and was greeted with a cheer: "Hurrah for Wilson; he kept us out of war!" It is said that in response he lifted his hand in solemn asseveration, saying: "Yes, and as long as Wilson is President you will stay out of war." He won the election on that plea; but the big moneyed States went against him. Meanwhile imperialistic Russia had slumped, the Czar had abdicated, and big loans made to the Allies by American millionaires who were willing to help on the devastation were said to be in danger. Big dailies with big money back of them set up a howl, and little dailies joined in. With Washington's words to guide him and with the precedents of the decades of our national existence to give him strength President Wilson was not able to stand. Like Walpole in the case of Jenkins' ear, rather than resign he yielded to the pressure and sent in his fateful message on the quixotic plea of making the world safe for democracy. After all the sacrifices that the people made, the world was not appreciably changed for the better; on the contrary democracy at home was so jeoparded that the government thought it wise to deport ship-loads of people at public expense, and President Wilson went to bed for months. The money grubber is always a menace to peace, when blood can be coined into cash and the cash invested in untaxable bonds bearing interest for thirty years.

There are also influential individuals who stand for war with all the degradations which it entails, Before the loss of his gallant and gifted son, a loss which the affectionate father did not long survive, Mr. Roosevelt scorned the idea of stopping war. He favoured large families, and said the mother who objected to rearing her son to be a soldier might as well object to rearing her daughter to be a mother, connecting war and sex again. He advocated the imperialistic Jap idea of putting the military in the public schools of the land and forcing every boy to go the gait, unless he was physically unfit. He was willing for the weak and frail to walk the ways of peace. His views are held by many others, who have adopted them second hand or worked them out for themselves.

In addition to these impressive facts there is no known government that has formally gone on record against war. On the contrary the popular item of expense in government budgets is the appropriation to cover the costs of war. It is said the late fury cost the British empire the astounding sum of forty thousand million pounds sterling, but the burden was assumed with enthusiasm. If anybody questioned the wisdom of it all, he was prob ably considered a traitor and dealt with accordingly. The British spirit prevails in other nations also. However averse to war on the part of others, each claims the right to wage war for itself, and in every case it judges its war to be just and righteous. And if this is the correct view, why all the talk about ending a thing that works righteousness among men?

Like the nations, the churches also stand for war. Mr. Wells says people whose sentiments outrun their knowledge assume that Christianity as it is known is an attempt to embody and enforce the personal teachings of Christ. Certainly this is what it ought to be; but he denies that it is anything of the kind, and challenges the proof from any church authority. On the contrary he says the chosen symbol of Christianity is the cross to which Jesus was nailed and on which he died. When the recent storm broke over Europe, and portions of Belgium and France were swept by the besom of destruction, some men in Congress de sired to express a formal protest and were duly suppressed by others in authority; but no church anywhere took the trouble to express any sort of regret over the things that were coming to pass.

Early in 1917 the matter was definitely brought to the attention of one of the larger Christian bodies in the following paper. Referring to the war that was engaging the nations it

"*Resolved*: 1. That we deeply deplore this awful and sorrowful calamity which has caused these leading nations to drench the earth in the precious blood of their own loyal citizens.

2. That we reaffirm our faith in the righteousness

of the Sermon on the Mount, and our confidence in the infallible wisdom of him who taught us to love our enemies, to bless them that curse us, and to do good to them that despitefully use and persecute us.

3. That we desire a stronger faith in God, who maketh wars to cease even to the ends of the earth, and we shall rejoice if our own people, and all of every name who love the Lord Jesus Christ in sincerity, shall find it in their hearts to pray for kings and for all that are in authority, that we may live quiet and peaceable lives in all godliness and honesty."

The meeting was composed of 1,683 members, representing a constituency of two millions and more. Only 112 voted for the resolutions. A storm of angry protest was raised, and the secular papers reported that the author of the paper, a man mature in years and known to the assembly, was hooted and hissed and threatened with personal violence by honourable members of the body. The incident illustrated what Professor Shaler said about the temper of crowds, that under conditions favourable to such a result a large company of perfectly respectable clergymen could be turned into a howling murderous mob. The case was typical of the church attitude toward war, though possibly exceptional in the degree of passion shown. Under stress of war animosity the minds of good men were warped, judgment was suspended and passion took the reins. So far as is recalled, not a single great religious body made any protest against the crimes of war, or expressed any regret for the desolation and misery it caused; on the contrary, many of them warmly endorsed it and pledged it their hearty support, every additional man flung into the mill only an addition to the work of destruction.

Knowing the facts in the case as they are, many intelligent and thoughtful persons can see no end to the desolations of war. They regard the forces that are for it as too strong to be overcome, and they are deeply depressed by the prospect. The lot of mankind seems almost hopeless. If every advance in scientific knowledge and mechanical skill is to mark greater efficiency in the destructive and brutal work of war, why shall the world struggle to advance? Why shall women suffer to bring forth sons simply to feed the hunger of the guns, or daughters to endure the agony which war inflicts? Why shall men bow their shoulders to crushing burdens and toil unto supreme weariness, if the products of their labour are to be swallowed up in bringing pang and ruin to the race? Why. not follow the course of some tribes in the war-stricken East, and lapse into primitive conditions in which the means of destruction are less effective?

There are some, however, who face the future with more hopefulness. Altars may be in ruins and prophets killed or driven into exile, the residue may be hated and hunted for their lives; but there are seven thousand and more who have not been swept down by the tide of passion, nor forced to bow the knee to the Baal of war nor to pollute their lips with his praise. There are devout souls who consider war ghostly and atrocious, and they are brave enough to oppose the war god and plan for his repudiation and final overthrow. It is a consummation devoutly to be wished.

This result cannot be accomplished through violence, be it never so frightful. There is a nursery tale about a simple enemy who tried to destroy Brer Rabbit by throwing him into the briar patch, but it is kept for children. Fighting the Devil with fire is a good way to vent spleen and work mischief; but there is no evidence that it hurts the Devil in any way. The student of history knows the vanity of such a course. From the day Cain slew Abel the method has been tested under all possible conditions, and its abortiveness has been fully disclosed.

According to the Gothic account the ancient Huns were the bastard progeny of impure women and unclean spirits. The women began their base career as attendants upon King Filimer's camps; becoming too cunning they were suspected of being witches and were driven out, but after their experience in the camps they found it easy to consort with demons. Attila was the rare result of such heredity. He hated all civilized men and scorned their accomplishments, but he found a way to use them in working out his nefarious designs. With cunning veiled behind a visage of rudeness, with excessive arrogance and beastly sensuality the little swarthy Kalmuck, as Hodgkin called him, won undying fame for his ruthless ferocity; but suddenly and mysteriously he died in a drunken slumber some fifteen centuries ago, and all his violence left no sign of ending violence in the earth.

There is an animal side to man, and the game animal does not quail in the presence of danger. The hen and all her progeny have never solved the simplest problem in Euclid, but a heroic rooster with both legs amputated above the spurs has been known to maintain his place in the pit, fighting like fury and crowing as he fought. The bear is neither a pacifist high brow nor the froth of too easy existence; though he has never written a poem or carved a statue, he is as brave as Richard Cœur de Lion or the modern French Tiger, and a heroic he bear properly aroused will fight a circular saw in motion. The cow is usually a peaceful creature; none of her tribe have ever risen to fame in art or literature, but there is a story abroad that a heroic bull once charged a moving locomotive. The horse is a useful beast. Although he has never discovered a planet nor painted a picture, the Bible bears testimony to his heroism. He mocketh at fear and is not affrighted, neither turneth he back from the sword. He rattleth the quiver and beareth the glittering spear and shield. He laugheth at the trumpets, the thunder of the captains and the shoutings, and swallowing the ground in the fierceness of his rage he goeth on to meet armed men. And in physical courage man is quite the equal of any beast.

An ignorant and criminal negro has been known to ride to the gallows on his own coffin without a tremor, guying other negroes on the road, assuring them that they need not hurry inasmuch as there would be no fun till he arrived. It was the unthinking animal dying game without any concern for the solemn issues involved in death. In the same spirit thousands have gone from the battle-field into eternity. True to his name,

> "Brave Wolfe drew up his men
>   In form so pretty,
> On the Plains of Abraham
>   Before the city;
> There just below the town
>   The French did meet them,
> And with double numbers
>   They resolved to beat them."

Beating, however, was a game that two could play, and the Wolfe knew the game. After a season of mutual slaughter the French ran away, but not til they had given the opposing leader a deadly wound. As the brave Wolfe lay bleeding to death, as bled the heroic bear that fought the deadly saw, he heard that the battered French were running away, and according to the admiring poet he said with his last gasp: "I die with pleasure." The heroic bear also died, but the voice that he uttered was in-articulate; neither did the heroic cock that fought after both legs were gone crow in definite terms, but the tone seemed jubilant.

Instead of being a terror to physical courage ferocity is a challenge, especially to those who in relative safety plan the savageries of war. For a moment there seemed to be some envy of the big gun, called Betsy, that hurled a deadly missile upon innocent people seventy-six miles away; but so soon as the opposition had time to recover from the amazement, it hastened to announce that it could make a gun to shoot a hundred miles, if it wanted to, going the Betsy twenty-four miles better. The deadlier the danger the finer the animal courage that defies it. The steeper and higher the embankment the more heroic the feat of going over the top, and for such as survive the richer the meaning of the iron cross, and the *croix de guerre*, and the bravery medal, and the brass button, and the military promotion, and the honourable mention, or any of the other valueless devices that have been invented to set a premium on expertness in human butchery.

To be sure, there have come vague rumours of brutal officers forcing reluctant men over the top with oaths and threats of death, the men going into the jaws of death afoot or otherwise with guns behind them as well as to the right and the left. There have also come suppressed whisperings of men who valued their lives and swooned away, sometimes going grey in an hour, sometimes going deranged in their minds and committing suicide, under the coercion that forced them over the top. Like the heroic mule that went to the bottom in the mining shaft, many of them had no choice in the matter; they were under the constraint of the conscript act, and were subject to military discipline, a gallows sometimes looming in sight. It was heroism by statutory enactment; the instincts of nature demanded that men preserve themselves, and obeying nature's behest to the limit they did their best. A rat sometimes fights for his life, when he is cornered.

People at a safe distance looked upon the frightfulness of going over the top almost as a joke. The slang of the battle-field became quite popular. It suddenly took high rank in the vocabulary of peace. Merchants went over the top in the sale of goods. Lawyers went over the top in successful causes before the courts. Politicians went over the top in seeking coveted positions. Preachers went over the top in their efforts to get more money. One man who stormed at the Lord much as a military officer roars at a subordinate was said to go over the top in his prayer. The case considered as a whole clearly shows that war cannot be ended by frightfulness. Cattle sometimes stampede, and the animal man sometimes gets panicky; but in the aggregate he cannot be scared into the ways of righteousness and peace. The scheme to end war by leagues and treaties is equally abortive and vain. It has been tested for centuries, and in every case it has failed when there was good reason for failure. Three hundred years before Christ the Congress of Corinth formed a League of Public Peace, which recognized Philip and later Alexander as its head. In due time some of the high contracting parties felt that their autonomy was abridged; they accordingly repudiated their treaty, and went to war. The battle was to the strong, and Alexander won. Their disregard of the treaty became a pretext for uncommon cruelty; many of them were brutally murdered, and the remnants were sold into slavery to meet the expenses of the war.

Rawlinson tells of what was boastfully called an Endless Peace solemnly effected between Rome and Persia in the year 532, which cost the emperor Justinian two and a half tons of gold. The vaunted peace that was never to end lasted just eight years. The thing that began in hypocrisy ended in treachery and falsehood according to the spirit of the war god.

The annals of the ages are replete with such abortions. Candid and capable men know that there has never been a treaty formed strong enough to bind people that have been swept by war passions and confronted by what is called military necessity. In the judgment of militarists such necessity quite justifies the breach of treaties, the abrogation of oaths, the suspension of constitutional provisions, the alienation of inalienable rights, the seizure of private property, and almost any other illegal act that fury seems to demand. Our own history furnishes ample testimony concerning these matters.

The authors of the proposed league of peace confess its futility. On leaving France Secretary Lansing said the instrument was not what he had hoped for. In his favourable judgment it left many problems unsettled, left out many things that ought to have been inserted, and put in things that ought to have been left out. President Wilson himself was constrained to confess it a league for war rather than peace. Speaking to the millions the *Saturday Evening Post* said no American was satisfied with it. Mindful of their oaths of office the majority of the Senate said it ought to be much modified, and some felt that it ought to be rejected altogether.

The proposal to abolish war by agreement is false in principle. If a million of merchants were to enter into an agreement not to swindle one another or their customers, it would be a confession that they were all thieves at heart. If a thousand lawyers were to propose a public covenant not to resort to doubtful methods in their practice, it would be proof positive that they were a thousand shysters. If a hundred matrons were to enter a solemn engagement not to betray their husbands, it would be a public scandal, and would surely start the divorce mill. If war is right and proper, a source of freedom and progress, a tonic for the nations and an uplift for the masses, a sure path to glory here and to heaven hereafter, as the junkers of every land have claimed, it ought to continue, and the talk about ending it or limiting its beneficent power is all wrong. If, on the contrary, war is a ghostly atrocity, as Dr. Truett has suggested, a crime against the poor and helpless, who are its chief victims, and a sin against the loving Father in heaven, it ought to come to an end; but it cannot be ended by agreement, because the minds of men can neither be coerced nor changed by contract.

If all the parties that enter a league against war honestly believe that war is right and helpful, they are disingenuous in proposing such a league. If any of them believe that war is wrong and hurtful, they show themselves moral cowards and ethical derelicts in offering to make their honest convictions a matter of contingency. The offer to do so indicates a condition of ethical decay.

Further, such a league is clearly, contrary to what God has revealed for the guidance of his own people. Of old there were ungodly nations on the earth, Philistines, Girgashites, Hittites, Hivites, Jebusites, Perizzites, and what not, quite as righteous as the Chinese, the Huns, the Japs, the Mexicans, the Turks, and others who inhabit the earth to-day; and God spoke unto his people through his servant Moses, saying: "Thou shalt make no covenant with them." He repeated the commandment and gave them warning: "Take heed to thyself, lest thou make a covenant with the inhabitants of the land"; and he explained the inhibition, assuring his people that such a league would bring them into trouble. Through the faithlessness of their leaders the people were beguiled into disobedience, and after the thing was done they tried to counteract the evil by bringing the Gibeonites with whom they were leagued into subjection and making them hewers of wood and drawers of water, but the mischief was done, and it marked the be ginning of the end.

There is not on earth to-day a nation chosen of God as Israel was chosen, nor is there a leader to whom God has spoken as he spoke to Moses; but there are multitudes of men and women who feel that they have been called by his Spirit, and are subject to his will. They receive the Bible as God's word to them, and in all good conscience they are obliged to object to any sort of league that binds them to submit to the judgment of ungodly peoples, whether Pagan, Mohammedan or subjects of other creeds.

The idea of a league of nations to force peace upon the world is of distinctly unchristian origin. Immanuel Kant, born in 1724, was the leading agnostic in Germany for many years. He proposed a league of nations bound by a covenant of its own to act through a congress or council for the regulation of all international matters. Jeremy Bentham, of London, took up the idea, and proposed a congress of deputies chosen from the nations to adjust international disputes, suggesting as a preliminary condition the reduction of military establishments and the abandonment of colonies by European nations. Both Kant and Bentham followed Thomas Hobbes, a deist of the seventeenth century, who did as much to discredit the principles of religion and morality as any man of his time. Hobbes regarded the passion for war as a fundamental human trait, every man by nature being at war with every other man. He saw security only in the suppression of the natural instinct. In his view the king, the ruling class, some delegated body was necessary to make decisions and enforce them against the evil inclinations of the coarse and unruly masses. Mr. Hobbes, however, was too frank and honest to offer such a scheme in the interest of democracy. He openly conceded that it meant subjection rather than freedom, a ruling class and a ruled class, overlords and underlings. It marked the end of equality, liberty, fraternity and all the distinctive elements of government by the people. Naturally it was a breeder of arrogance and oppression on the part of those who held the places of authority. Even in the domain of religion that sort of power to dominate the wills of men and dictate their actions impelled a bishop to assume a triple crown and claim to be king of earth and also of heaven and hell. Instead of ending war such a scheme put the question of making war entirely in the hands of a few ambitious men. It was a menace rather than a defense, and the world did not adopt it.

Neither can the world look to the formal and functional thing called historic Christianity for relief. In 1917 the only considerable areas on the globe that were not shadowed by the ominous clouds of war and swept by the savage passion for blood were found in darkest heathenism. Thoughtful men outside the Church, Agnostics, Jews, unbelievers of various schools, quietly noted the failure of Christianity, and were confirmed in their unbelief. Many trembling spirits in the churches were shaken with doubt, and began to question the reality of their faith. The strenuous efforts that church people made to do something – to syndicate their forces, to perfect an organization, to kindle enthusiasm, to gather millions of money, to get a new hold, to seize a passing opportunity, to save a situation, were the instinctive struggles of men who felt that they were sinking. It all indicated failure rather than success, and excited a smile from the worldly crowd represented by such publications as *Life*.

This side the sea there will probably be no question that nominal Christianity failed in Germany, the land of Luther and the boasted reformation. It was a form of Christianity flowering out in a spirit that put devotion to country above devotion to the teachings of Christ, or else confounded the two, and invariably pledged support to the government in the bloody and destructive work of war. In some parts the Church named for the great re former felt constrained to disavow fellowship with the German emperor, but in so doing it equally disavowed fellowship with German Christianity which gave him loyal support in his atrocious work.

The failure was equally conspicuous in Austria and Hungary, where almost the entire population was reckoned as Christian, Church and state being practically coextensive. Like the Germans, the people of those lands accepted the Turks as allies and comrades in the savageries of war and vied with them in ruthlessness. Their thin veneer of Christianity, to use the Archdeacon's phrase, conformed to Mohammed's teaching rather than to Christ's, and added fury to their ungodly work. It was the same type of Christianity that moved in the hearts of their Italian enemies, and it made the border streams run with human blood. The same also that instigated the atrocities of Louis xiv and the barbarities of the Spanish Philip ii. And there is not an intelligent and unbiased mind on earth that will pronounce it a true form of Christian faith.

Bishop William Ingraham Kip claims that the Gospel was introduced into Britain in the days of the apostles, and that the name of Christ was honoured on the banks of the Thames, when even in the city of

Rome Christianity was considered a pernicious super-stition. Whether the Bishop's claim is exact or not, true Christianity was known in England at a very early date. To-day more than half the people who muster under the British flag are Agnostics and Jews and Mohammedans, and with all these the veneer Christians of the empire joined heartily in all the bloody and destructive work of war, fighting with equal fury and giving equal welcome to Pagan allies from Japan. Whatever the differences in their speech, they were all moved by the same spirit. It was the spirit of hatred and violence that fired the passions of Austrians, Germans, Hungarians, Poles, Russians, Servians, Turks, Czechs and all the rest. It was the spirit that led into the way of erring Israel, and trusted in might and power to win; and it was not the Spirit of God.

Through some fifteen centuries France has known the name of Jesus. Almost from the beginning of the art of printing she has had some access to the Bible. In recent times the Scriptures have been free to circulate in all the land. In Paris alone there are scores of learned societies organized for the purpose of research in various branches of human investigation; the famous Latin Quarter is simply an aggregation of students and schools centering about the great University, centuries old and known throughout the world, and French mathematicians and scientists are unsurpassed. But ten thousand witnesses can be found to give testimony that the formal Christianity of France has failed. Soldiers who were forced across on the pretext of saving civilization reluctantly admit that what they found in moral and spiritual life was hardly worth saving. Some of the disillusioned preachers who quit their pulpits and went off to aid in the brutal work of war have returned seriously talking of sending missionaries from America, which was inhabited by savages when Paris was flourishing in the light of high civilization, to show cultured Parisians how to be Christians!

What Church will send the missionaries? Following the example of Peter the German the churches that are able to put up the millions to pay their proxies have formally committed themselves to what Lyman Abbott calls the twentieth-century crusade, and have gone forth to establish righteousness and peace by violence and blood. If France is in need of righteousness, why not send soldiers and guns rather than missionaries and Bibles? Or will the missionaries be instructed to follow the example of the German Charles, so admired by the French as to be appropriated as Charlemagne, and offer the alternative of getting religion or being killed and sent on to h–l? Or if they are instructed to abandon the policy of violence and leave their guns behind, after they learn the melody of Parisian speech what will they teach? Will they try to explain that there is one gospel for times of war and another for times of peace? Will they confess that the doctrine of righteousness by violence is wrong, or will they ignore the subject entirely as if nothing had happened, trust the French to do the same, and proceed to preach the gospel of kindness and love, which they all alike have failed to practice? Will they make their appeal to the French heart by the love of Jesus, who died an ignominious death at the hands of his enemies instead of resorting to force, or will they plead the fact that they aided the French in hating and killing their enemies? It will be an interesting spectacle, and certainly some one can be hired to undertake the work; but the gospel of violence has failed in the past, and the future is easy to predict.

What distinctive quality can American Christianity offer the Christianity of France or Germany or Russia or any other of the bleeding countries of Europe? They have all shown the same spirit and have used the same methods. Generally in Europe the Church was bound up with the state, and when the state went to war the Church was necessarily in it; but in America the case was different. The Church boasted of its freedom from state control. It was bound by the word of Jesus to render unto Cæsar the things that were Cæsar's, but Cæsar made no demand on it. Its participation in the bloody work of war was entirely voluntary. It left Jesus out of its war councils, and deliberately rendered unto Cæsar the things it had dedicated unto God. Like the hands of its brethren in France or Germany or elsewhere in wretched Europe, its hands also are full of blood. Its tongue is quite as profane and vituperative as theirs. All alike have adopted the heathen idea of doing evil that good may come. All alike have hated and killed their enemies, and have fought with equal fury side by side with Japs and Turks. But the American church was separate from the state, and was not forced into the strife; it simply pushed itself in. How will it feel in proposing to pull the mote out of its European brother's eye, when, behold, a beam is in its own eye?

From unreal premises no positive conclusion can, be drawn. The thoughtful man will not undertake to affirm what would be, if things were not as they are. But there is a realm of legitimate speculation. Analogies are not conclusive, but they are suggestive. Facts somehow force inferences, and the pages of Christian history preserve some impressive facts.

Christianity dawned upon a faithless and wicked world. It was a world grim with hatred, and bleeding from many wounds. It was weary and heavy laden and furious in its helplessness. Its philosophies engaged the educated classes, but had no sway over the masses of mankind, and no balm for the wounds of their devotees. The Stoic said there was no escape, and men must learn to suffer and be strong. The Epicurean said it was best to eat and drink and drown pain in sensuous delight. The Sadducee said the race was to the swift and the battle to the strong, and there was neither guardian angel nor helping spirit to aid in the strife. The Christian told a different tale. He proclaimed a Father God, who revealed himself in the person of his Son Christ Jesus the Lord. He taught those who hated and destroyed one another that they were brethren of one blood; he bade them bear one another's burdens and so fulfill the law of Christ, and he illustrated his doctrine in his own life. The Church held in a common bond of love the rich and the poor, the wise and the unwise. The church members were in the world, but they were not of the world. They did not separate themselves from their kind, but they lived a different life. They were smitten, but they did not smite. They were reviled, but they reviled not again. They were cursed, but they blessed in return. They did not kill their enemies; they prayed for them. They were living epistles known and read by sinners around them, and their message of peace and love prevailed. It was a message which the world was willing to hear.

In less than thirty years after Pentecost Christianity was a distinct power in all Palestine and Syria and Asia Minor, and in Imperial Rome there was a church whose faith was spoken of throughout the whole world. It took the Apostle Paul only three weeks to set up a church at Thessalonica, which has as nearly a consecutive history down to the present time as any such organization on earth. In other European cities there were strong and triumphant churches. The wall of partition which had separated people of different tribes and tongues was broken down, and there were saints in Cæsar's household.

From the best available data Vedder estimates that in seventy years from the beginning there were not fewer than a hundred thousand Christian men and women living in the empire, while thousands more had passed on to their reward. Early in the second century Pliny wrote to the Emperor Trajan that the superstition, as he called it, had pervaded not only the cities of his province, but also the villages and the farms, so that the heathen temples were almost deserted and the heathen rites in neglect. And it seems a reasonable inference that if the Church had remained true to the teachings of Jesus, it would have driven out the spirit of hatred and strife, and would have dominated the world before now.

Thoughtful men of different classes freely concede that if the teachings of Jesus had gripped and held Europe in 1914, the fury that desolated the nations would not have come. Henry Watterson, not a church member, but a man wise by long experience and by a deep knowledge of his own soul, says the paramount issue underlying democracy and everything else of real value is the doctrine of Christ and him crucified. He declares that if the world is to be saved from physical and spiritual destruction it must be done through the teachings of Jesus. Without that teaching and influence he sees only the prospect of eternal war. In the same strain the *Wall Street Journal* pleads for a genuine revival of religion as the country's supreme need. Other testimony outside the Church is equally strong.

In what he calls a parting message to the world the late Earl Grey, Governor General of Canada, says there is a real way out of the mess into which materialism has plunged the nations, and it is Christ's way, which he says he urged for thirty years: "We've got to give up quarreling. We've got to come together. We've got to realize that we are members of the same family. There is nothing that can help humanity, I am sure there is nothing, perfectly sure, except love. Love is the way up." It is a noble sentiment nobly uttered, and it is worthy of a great soul standing at the gate of eternity. It clearly points the way, and from the universal Christian conscience unbiased by passion it evokes approving response.

Don C. Seitz frankly expresses the opinion that peace on earth based upon justice between man and man will never come. He bases his opinion on the idea that no nation will be brave enough, brave enough is his phrase, to put down its arms, and dismantle its warships, and abandon its war schools, and proclaim to the world that it will not wallow in the filth of war; that no nation will have the moral courage to do right, and let others take the consequences of their own wrong-doing. Ancient Israel had absolute assurance of protection without resorting to war on their own responsibility, but the red-blooded fellows among them, the kind that have so boasted of their prowess in recent times, were not satisfied with the divine plan, and they rejected God to be like the heathen. Through the ages the heathen idea of protection by might has prevailed in all nations.

Since that day of rejection God has not called any nation to do his will. Whether invisible on the eternal throne or manifest in the flesh God has chosen to work through individuals. Judas may betray and Peter deny and others grow panicky and flee, but he changes not. He has infinite leisure for the accomplishment of his holy designs.

> "His purposes will ripen fast,
> Unfolding every hour."

In power as resistless as the tides he will work his sovereign will. He shall not cry aloud in rage, nor lift up a shout of defiance, neither shall his voice be heard in clamour and tumult on the streets. A crushed reed shall he not break down in fury, a flickering wick shall he not snuff out in impatience, but in undisturbed quiet he shall bring forth judgment unto truth. Whatever the doubt and failure of his frail disciples, he shall not fail nor be discouraged concerning his plans until he shall establish peace in all the earth. And he shall win not by armies nor by battle with confused noise and garments rolled in blood, but by the power of the truth quickened by the Holy Ghost.

The apostle says there must needs be a falling away, that the man of sin may be revealed. In the appalling slump that has come in the last few years that wicked one, who is destined to destruction by the divine word, has been fully disclosed in all his frightfulness, and every discerning eye has seen. Yielding for a time to leaders blinded by passion the people have gone into the ditch, but the masses of God's people are true at heart. In the darkest hours there is always a remnant according to the election of grace, and Jesus is the same forever more.

Of old when men failed to lead the people aright, God found courage and faith in a woman, in Deborah a mother in Israel. By his providence he is again calling women to assume larger responsibilities and to give additional aid in solving the problems of the times and in saving the world from threatened ruin. In days of passion they will not justify Kipling's sneer, that the female of the species is as deadly as the male. The vast majority of them are disciples of the meek and lowly. Jesus. They will not imitate the heathen women of Sparta and Philistia and dedicate their children to the god of war and cause them to go through the fire, but they will dedicate them to the God of Peace, and lead them in the ways of righteousness. They love the Lord, and like Ann Askew, and Joan Catmer, and Elizabeth Cooper, and Alice Driver, and Jane Gray, and Margaret Hide, and Catherine Knight, and Joan Lashford, and Alicia Lyle, and Agnes Snoth, and Joan Sole and many others who laid down their lives rather than betray their Lord, these thousands of Christian women will withstand the power of the false teachers, the junkers and the money grubbers, and will be true to the spirit and teachings of Jesus Christ. It is the beginning of better things.

Under the guidance of leaders who have the moral courage to be true to Christ and his word now, Judas will depart and hang himself, Peter will repent in tears and will receive Pentecostal power, the panicky ten will recover their faith and will take their place by their suffering Master, Thomas and other doubters will rise above the mists that have obscured their vision, and Christian people will recognize the full authority of their Lord. Instead of waiting for Turks and Huns and others who know not God to find and lead the way, they will gladly stand in the place of their absent Lord, who has intrusted his presence in the world to them. They will look for his return, and will not have him find their hands red in the blood of their enemies, when he comes. In meekness of spirit they will teach every man his neighbour and every man his brother man to know the Lord who speaks peace to the nations and extends his dominion from sea to sea. It will be a welcome message, the old message sounded in the day of the Church's triumph, and men will hear and heed.

"Then shall wars and tumults cease;
Then be banished grief and pain;
Righteousness and joy and peace,
Undisturbed shall ever reign."

AMEN.

www.ingramcontent.com/pod-product-compliance
Lightning Source LLC
Chambersburg PA
CBHW032134020426
42334CB00016B/1158